SUDHIR CHOUDHRIE

FROM MY HEART

A Tale of Life, Love and Destiny

JOHN BLAKE

Published by John Blake Publishing Ltd
3 Bramber Court, 2 Bramber Road,
London W14 9PB, England

www.johnblakebooks.co.uk

www.facebook.com/johnblakebooks ⓕ
twitter.com/jblakebooks ⓣ

First published in hardback in 2017

ISBN: 978 1 78606 389 2

British Library Cataloguing-in-Publication Data:

A catalogue record for this book is available from the British Library.

Design by www.envydesign.co.uk

Printed in Great Britain by CPI Group (UK) Ltd

1 3 5 7 9 10 8 6 4 2

Papers used by John Blake Publishing are natural, recyclable products made
from wood grown in sustainable forests. The manufacturing processes
conform to the environmental regulations of the country of origin.

Every attempt has been made to contact the relevant copyright-holders,
but some were unobtainable. We would be grateful if the
appropriate people could contact us.

For my wife Anita, and for my donor

CONTENTS

	FOREWORD	IX
CHAPTER 1	A HEART FLIES IN	1
CHAPTER 2	A GILDED CHILDHOOD	17
CHAPTER 3	BROTHERHOOD	33
CHAPTER 4	I HAD FORGOTTEN HOW BEAUTIFUL ANITA IS	49
CHAPTER 5	THE HEART BEGINS TO BREAK	65
CHAPTER 6	MY BROTHER, RAJIV	79
CHAPTER 7	THE HEART OF THE MATTER	95
CHAPTER 8	A NEW HEART AWAKES	113
CHAPTER 9	HEART ACHE	131
CHAPTER 10	BAD DREAMS	149
CHAPTER 11	COME FLY WITH ME	165

CHAPTER 12   LIFE, ACTUALLY   183

CHAPTER 13   FATHER TO A COMPANY   199

CHAPTER 14   TO GIVE IS GREATER   205
             THAN TO RECEIVE

CHAPTER 15   A HEART'S DESIRE   219

DR DONNA MANCINI'S SPEECH – TENTH
ANNIVERSARY OF SUDHIR'S TRANSPLANT   231

SUDHIR CHOUDHRIE PROFESSORSHIP OF
CARDIOLOGY LECTURE BY DR. OZ   239

FOREWORD

It gave a piteous groan, and so it broke;
In vain it something would have spoke:
The love within too strong for 't was,
Like poison put into a Venice-glass.

'The Heart Breaking' by Abraham Cowley

Poets frequently write of the human heart, often using monikers like courageous or broken or bleeding or cold or stone. The term 'big' is also frequently and innocently applied, but to a heart surgeon like me this is a deadly accusation. Unfortunately, the description perfectly described Sudhir 'Bunny' Choudhrie's heart when I met him in a hospital bed in Columbia Medical Center in New York on a Friday night in 1999. I was tired from a long week of surgery, but the cardiology team had insisted that I meet Bunny that evening. His family had been cursed with a genetic abnormality that had already stolen his brother's life prematurely. Bunny was next in line and lay listless, having trouble processing so much bad news in such a short period of time. His belly was swollen from the backlog of ascites fluid from his engorged heart. This put extra pressure on his lungs which were already drowning in edema, like a waterlogged sponge. His blood pressure was maintained only with a high-octane concoction of medications dreamt up by my world famous colleague, cardiologist Dr Donna Mancini. Thankfully Bunny's wife Anita stood at his side like Venus de Milo in a sari and started peppering me with questions about the future of her beloved. I offered mostly monosyllabic answers.

Would he die without surgery? Yes.

How long did he have? Hours to days.

Was replacing his heart the only option? Yes.

How risky was the operation? Fifty-fifty.

Her decisions were precise and clear. We should try to transplant Bunny immediately and she would ensure everyone would support whatever was needed to ensure this happened, in particular keeping Bunny emotionally engaged to fight through a very difficult operation and recovery.

Luck favours the prepared mind, but sometimes you also have to be just plain lucky. Bunny continued to deteriorate over the weekend, but he stayed alive just long enough for us to identify a suitable heart. The details of his harrowing surgery and recovery are a main focus of this book. Upon opening his chest, his heart appeared like a swollen tic and only grudgingly budged to pump miniscule amounts of blood to Bunny's starved body. The new heart was a coiled python, squeezing and compressing every red blood cell out into the body to deliver its life sustaining oxygen. These are the exciting moments that capture our imagination and inspired me to follow heart surgery as a career. But let me focus my foreword on the even more important issues: why Bunny survived and why his desire to write a memoir is worthy of our attention.

Life happens when we are busy making plans. Facing death awakens us to this reality. When Bunny peered over the towering cliff of life into the dark abyss of death, he made two promises: he would stay calm in the face of adversity and he would live life to the fullest for every remaining day on this stage if he survived. Bunny kept both his promises. During the operation and its recovery, Bunny would often point out that worrying about outcomes doesn't help much and takes up too much Qi, which tends to be a scarce resource when you are fighting for your life. Bunny appreciated early in his illness that battling death is a marathon rather than a wind sprint, so our precious energy has to be focused on areas that make a difference, like taking a deep breath in the ICU or an extra step in rehab.

Once he fully recovered, Bunny re-engaged with life with a vice-like grip to ensure that his friends, associates, and beloved family felt his positive presence every day. He lives in the moment at every moment because he acutely felt the pain of having very few moments left. The wisdom gained from a life lived with these insights is worth sharing and I applaud Bunny's commitment to seeing this task through to its enjoyable finish, like most everything else he has touched in the last decade and a half. After all, despite a kind donor who gave him a gift of life, he is still living on borrowed time. His donor is the real anonymous hero of Bunny's story, and the donor family's heroic act enabled the heroes of this book, Bunny and Anita, to pass it on. And they took this opportunity to continually touch the lives of so many in the unique ways described later in this memoir. They capture the essence of the tale in this elegant paragraph nestled at the end of the story:

'Of course, at the heart of it all, this is a love story. Hearts have broken in this tale – more than one of them, and emotionally as well as physically – but they have been mended too. The hearts belonging to the family of my donor must have been shattered by their loss and yet they rose above their grief to say yes to the procedure that gave me life. My heart, my new heart, swells with a profound emotion at that thought.'

Now turn the page and get ready for a rollercoaster ride.

Dr Mehmet Oz
7 February 2016

'Life is beautiful, full of love.
Live every moment to the full.'
SUDHIR CHOUDHRIE

CHAPTER I

A HEART
FLIES IN

It was a blisteringly cold January morning in New York City in the last year of the last millennium and the sky had turned a shade of early morning frozen blue, icy and pitiless, mirroring the frozen expanse of the city below. My wife Anita, exhausted after more than a week of sleepless nights but knowing that matters were finally to be resolved one way or another, stood in the atrium of Columbia University Medical Center. In the distance, through the huge glass windows, she could see a tiny speck on the horizon. As she watched, it grew bigger and bigger until it became obvious it was a helicopter, the rotors growing and growing in size as it neared the hospital below.

Placed as she was in the soundproof enclosure, Anita

couldn't hear the helicopter but she could see it as it neared and she knew exactly what cargo it was carrying: a heart. My heart. I do not to this day know where the heart came from or from whom, but lying elsewhere in the hospital that morning I too knew that my heart was approaching and I knew that this operation was make or break. After a lifetime of health problems, mainly prompted by a leaky valve in my heart that had been discovered when I was a child, the heart I was born with was no longer fit for purpose. After months of increasing ill-health, culminating in a medical collapse several weeks previously, my old heart had all but given up. The transplant, which had been predicted by the doctors for years now, was finally about to take place and my life now hung in the balance. And, at the eleventh hour, a replacement had been found.

Down in the depths of the hospital, just before I was rushed into the operating theatre where I was to receive my new heart, I had a conversation with my elder son Bhanu. He was then just twenty-one, still at college and was having to take on more responsibility than would otherwise have been the case at that tender age. As Bhanu remembers it, while Anita was watching life approaching the hospital from above, down below, we were talking about death. My death. Although I was determined that I would survive the forthcoming operation – as I had been throughout previous health scares in my life – it was a very high-risk procedure, with the danger that my body could reject the heart at any moment. This meant I had to talk to my son about what would happen to my family and the business I had spent decades building up with my beloved late brother Rajiv if I didn't make it through. 'It was a very difficult conversation,' Bhanu recalled years later. 'My father told me that he was going in to surgery, but he didn't know if he was coming out. He began to recount what was essentially his will in one of the most difficult and emotional conversations I have ever had.' Bhanu has a calm disposition and demeanour but even now, sixteen years on, it is a memory that still causes him a great deal of pain.

Most of my immediate family was there in Columbia: Anita, Bhanu, my mother Amrit and my cousin Sumant. My younger son Dhairya, who was still at school, remained in India, as did my nephew Dhruv, Rajiv's son, who was also now heavily involved in the family business. He too was waiting anxiously for developments: he had not been able to fly out to New York with us because someone needed to stay in Delhi to oversee the running of the company and the only possible candidate was him. But his concern was all the greater, as was that of the rest of the family, because by a dreadful coincidence, I had lost my very much beloved brother Rajiv less than a year earlier. He had also been experiencing heart problems and had also been waiting for a new heart. It was a devastating blow for me and all the family. My brother and I had been extremely close throughout my entire life – I was two years his junior but my daughter-in-law Simrin, Bhanu's wife, describes us as being 'akin to identical twins' – and his loss brought on an all-consuming grief to us all. He had been treated at Columbia, too, and I was told afterwards that the team, headed by the world-famous cardiothoracic surgeon Dr Mehmet Oz, who was about to operate on me, felt that they had lost one member of my family and were thus doubly determined to save his brother. But my family had been very badly affected by Rajiv's passing only a year earlier and it compounded the sense of helplessness and uncertainty that they all felt as my own operation approached.

I had been aware of the fact that I had health issues since I was a young child when, after a routine medical inspection for insurance purposes, it emerged that my heart had a leaky valve. Back then in India there was nothing we could do about it – this was the 1950s – but the family believed, accurately as it turned out, that one day the medical technology would exist that would provide the treatment I would come to need, although the idea of a heart being transplanted from one body into another would have been almost inconceivable back then. In fact, in many ways it still was unusual when it happened. I was at Columbia because it offered the best medical facilities in the world, but it is also true that the procedure could still not have been carried out in India at that time. Most people living on the sub-continent would have been astounded if they knew such a procedure could even take place.

But it was now essential. During the intervening years after that early childhood prognosis, I suffered from many more health problems, which I will detail later in this book, including an operation to replace the faulty valve. But it had become increasingly clear that I was going to need a full heart transplant and the crisis, when it happened, happened fast.

In December 1998, eight months after Rajiv's death, my health began to deteriorate very quickly, something Anita became aware of faster than I did myself. 'You had had a cough for six months and you couldn't get rid of it,' she recalls now. 'I was also increasingly aware that you were having a problem with water retention. You were still travelling a great deal but I could tell from your gait and your mannerisms that problems were growing. That December it got considerably worse and as the New Year approached I insisted that you see a doctor in New Delhi. He gave you a diuretic to reduce the extra fluid in the body, put you on medication and asked you to stay in hospital. You stayed just one night and then wanted to leave. I took you home and made sure you were comfortable, but then I returned on my own to the hospital, because I had heard the doctor use the phrase "heart failure". I went back to the doctor and asked, "What do you mean?"' Although Anita didn't say much to me about it at the time, I subsequently learned that she had become increasingly concerned for months and had quietly set about educating herself as to the nature of my condition and what would one day have to be done. And now that day was upon us.

In the meantime I could increasingly see something was wrong: quite apart from physical weakness, water was pouring out of my body, mainly through the soles of my feet. I was becoming more and more bloated – a direct result of my kidneys not functioning properly – and my general physical condition was worsening fast. The loss of Rajiv compounded all of this. Throughout my entire life I had had my brother to turn to in times of crisis both for advice and support, but now, when my heart was finally giving out on me, my brother wasn't there. My heart had been broken in more ways than one.

I had of course long been aware that one day I might need a transplant, but the normal human reaction to such a situation is not to think about it, not to believe it will ever actually happen, to put it out of your head by saying that it's something that might happen five years down the line. Now, however, it was becoming a reality, something I had to face and which could be postponed no longer. When the crunch came, I really was extremely ill and even though my heart was failing and I felt the need to talk to Bhanu about the future, at no point did I actually think I was really going to die. I studied astrology in my youth and I didn't believe that this was to be my destiny or my fate and on top of that I have been blessed with a very positive personality, always able to look to the future and determined to make the best of a bad situation. But as it became even clearer that something was very wrong, both my sons took it very hard. I could tell they were suffering but at that point there was no way of alleviating it. Bhanu was, as I previously mentioned, at college and Dhairya, not much older than a child, was still at school. Both were forced to witness a very quick physical deterioration in their father – something any child of any age would find difficult to deal with – and their pain was not diluted by our knowledge that one day this day would come.

After that initial appointment, Anita didn't tell me about the doctor's prognosis but she realised the extent to which I was seriously ill and started making the arrangements to fly to New York to see the specialists who had treated Rajiv. A doctor named Parvez Ahmed had been visiting from New York, and so we asked him if he would make the journey with us. In the meantime the state of my health was becoming quite critical and so the family assembled with due speed; with my sons and mother, we made arrangements to travel to New York via the UK.

January in New Delhi is a time of the year when the city is famous for its mists and fog. Flights are regularly delayed because the weather is absolutely dreadful, and this did indeed happen, necessitating a stay at a hotel airport, but we finally got on a BA flight to London. Time was becoming of the essence.

My body was continuing to swell because my kidneys weren't working properly and were unable to process any food or liquid. My doctor too was quite shocked when he saw the full extent of my problems with water retention because, throughout that gruesome journey, water continued to pour from the soles of my feet. Dr Ahmed was controlling my fluid intake throughout the various flights, but by this time I didn't feel like eating or drinking anything anyway and was barely aware of what was going on around me. It was becoming a blur, with the flight taking on the quality of a nightmare. The rest of the family was increasingly restive and anxious, with the tension building and the uncertainty and fear taking their toll. On the one hand this was a period of intense drama; on the other I was almost unaware of what was happening around me as the plane flew on, taking me to meet my destiny on the other side of the world.

After an overnight stay in London, we flew on to New York. Anita had arranged with the New York Medical Center to send an ambulance to the airport when we landed on 9 January, in the middle of the freezing New York winter – not that I was up to noticing the weather. I had previously been treated at that hospital and they took me straight to their ICU, where various blood tests were taken. This was increasingly difficult: I had become so bloated that they almost had to cut into the skin to make the incision, but it had to be done. The fact that it was a far more traumatic procedure than a normal blood test only served to highlight the horror of the whole situation. From there I was taken to Columbia and the wait began to find a suitable heart.

By this time, as I said, I was all but unaware of what was going on around me, but my family knew exactly what was happening. There was nothing any of us could do except wait for a heart. And it was taking a terrible toll. Both of my sons have related how they felt a terrible sense of powerlessness as I lay in hospital, barely conscious or able to move, although of course Dhairya was not on hand to witness it in person, as he was thousands of miles away in Delhi. 'The overriding feeling was of complete helplessness,' Bhanu recalls now. 'You can have everything material in life but at that point nothing mattered except for a team of doctors who have to make the forthcoming surgery successful. Nothing can prepare you for such a feeling and such a situation, when you see the person before you, your own father, essentially dying. It was the most emotional and saddest point in my life. What made it even worse was that you were facing the unknown but what you did know was what had happened the previous year, namely that his brother Rajiv, my uncle, had been in an extremely similar situation and we all knew how that had ended. It was a horrible, awful experience, but the one thing you could say about it was that it ultimately brought us all closer together.'

But still there was nothing we could do except wait for a suitable heart. Bhanu dealt with the uncertainty and anxiety by remaining active, dividing his time between our hotel and the hospital where he would constantly be checking with the doctors when they would be able to perform the surgery. Other family members came in to find out how it was all going, and there were frequent phone calls to Dhairya to keep him up to date with what was happening.

The situation was now even worse. The initial hope that the problem revolved around my replaced valve had collapsed entirely, which is why I needed to be transferred to Columbia, where I critically needed a heart. Bhanu and Sumant took up residence outside the office of Dr Donna Mancini, who had treated Rajiv and who was soon to be looking after me, to demand to know when I would be admitted prior to being assessed for the transplant list. At first no bed was available but everyone, including Dr Mancini, persisted in searching and I was shortly afterwards admitted. Now we just needed to be assessed and put on the list for my new heart.

But Anita, sensing my need for her despite the fact that I was barely conscious, never left Columbia during that interminable wait. She lived off sandwiches in the canteen and because there were no chairs in Intensive Care, perfected the art of standing by my bed for hours on end by shifting her weight from one foot to the other. She became like a bird, she says, able to take quick naps throughout the day, before snapping back to becoming fully alert. Eventually she was allowed a bed on the twelfth floor, where a few rooms were put aside for the family of critical patients from abroad and where Bhanu would also stay. The doctors were still running a battery of tests and I was sliding in and out of consciousness, and while I faintly recall an intense thirst, I was not allowed to drink anything. All that the doctors would agree to was a touch of ice on the mouth or a very tiny sip.

During that period of waiting, my family was interviewed in order to find out, essentially, whether I was a suitable candidate for a heart. For obvious reasons, good, healthy hearts do not often become available and when they do, doctors have to make a case as to why their patient, rather than anyone else's, should be the recipient. So the family were asked about everything: did I smoke or drink, to which the answer to both was 'no'; did I take drugs ('no');

was I the sole earner, that last question being to ascertain the importance of my role in the family. We were even asked where we lived. Anita had to go in front of a panel of doctors to answer all these questions and it quickly became clear that to be worthy of a new heart, you had to be on a kind of A-list to qualify.

The doctors didn't want patients who smoked or drank as their new heart would deteriorate quickly and deprive someone else, someone who might have gone on to have a better quality of life if they were treated, of a new chance of life. But this created a new layer of tensions all of its own and as with a great deal else at that time, Anita bore the brunt of the pressure. 'For me, the American system when it comes to transplants was completely new,' Anita recalls now. 'It made me so apprehensive and nervous in case I made an error or a mistake which meant Sudhir would not be taken on as a patient to have this operation.'

Because I was in a state of semi-consciousness, Anita recalls this period better than I do. And despite the worry and the strain, like me, she too had a very strong sense that I was going to survive the ordeal. 'I felt very strongly that Sudhir's destiny was to survive this crisis, but very unusually for him he let me take charge of everything at that point,' she says. 'I also knew that the doctors had never before done an operation on a patient with an artificial valve, as Sudhir had, and that the success rate for these types of operations generally was low. But I was sure he would survive. On the crucial day of the decision making, Dr Oz came into the room to see Sudhir and found him surrounded by his family – his wife, his mother and his son. Later he told us that when he saw us there, it took him back to his own family in his native Turkey. He could see how important this man was for all of us and there and then determined that he would do something.'

On the night of 16 January 1999, Anita was persuaded to go to her room and rest. Bhanu also stayed in the hospital that night, and the nurses attempted to calm mother and son, promising them that they would be alerted the moment anything happened. Neither could sleep properly but both had managed to doze off very briefly when the phone rang quite suddenly at four o'clock the following morning. 'Bhanu and I woke up with a terrible jolt and my son was quite grey,' Anita recalls. 'He just froze. There was a moment of complete panic, but the nurses said, "Mrs Choudhrie, there is very good news. Dr Oz has found a heart for your husband. He would like to see you so please come to his office. We rushed to Intensive Care to Dr Oz's room: a nurse was outside and gave me a big thumbs-up. My legs felt like wood; I could barely move as I was in such a state of shock, but I made it to Dr Oz's office with Bhanu at my side.

'It was still very early morning, completely dark, but

there was a light shining inside as he looked up at me from his desk. "Guess what?" he said quietly. "I've found you a heart." He'd had to fight for this: there is a pooled system that operates across all the hospitals, each of whom puts in a request for a heart. But Dr Oz had made a very, very strong case.'

And so, Anita went up to the atrium to wait for my heart as the doctors started to prepare for the operation, which was to start a couple of hours later. 'And I saw the helicopter arrive,' she recalls. 'I was totally focused on it and I was praying, all the time praying. But I knew it was Sudhir's destiny to survive. Somehow I knew there was a life after this: I never felt this was the end. The driving point for me always was, it wasn't meant to be like this for my husband. His destiny was different. I knew it would be fine. It was awful, of course, seeing him so vulnerable. But I always felt a stronger and greater force was with him and me.' She became increasingly emotional as she saw the paramedics take the cold box out of the helicopter containing its precious cargo and realised a great deal of activity was now taking place outside the operating theatre. This was the moment we had been awaiting for so very long.

In New York, everyone in the family was told straight away that a heart had been found and the operation was about to take place. Everyone in India was also informed. Dhairya vividly remembers when he discovered that I was finally going in for the transplant, as well as the feelings of isolation he experienced at being apart from the rest of his family during this difficult time. 'I was in India, at home in my room, when I got a phone call saying you were about to have a transplant,' he recalls now. 'I felt extremely shocked. A whole realm of emotions kicked in: I was upset and concerned, not least because we had already been through the operation where Dad's valve was replaced and after that there was the tragedy of my uncle dying. I was just seventeen and felt so conflicted about what I should do. I had just had some exam results when I got the call and this was the year of my GCSEs: I knew my parents wanted me to study and so I had to stay there. But until then I think I had been a little naïve about what was going to happen. I knew the situation was serious, of course, but the reality of what was going on didn't hit until I heard that the transplant really was going to take place.'

Unbeknownst to me, this operation had been in the pipeline throughout most of my life but I am certain that it was the enormous grief and pain I felt after Rajiv's death that had directly contributed to the final collapse of my own health and the fact that like my elder brother, I too needed a new heart. I was not the only person whose health had been affected by my brother's death: my mother – who also lost her husband, my father Shanti Prasad Choudhrie, when he was very young – was all but destroyed by it. She keeps a picture of Rajiv by her side, although she never mentions his name.

And I fear that the toll it took on her health when she discovered her other son, namely me, also needed a heart transplant, was too much for her to bear, to the extent that it has ended by destroying her health completely. But I was determined to survive; throughout all the health problems in my life, I have always been determined to survive and, barely conscious as I was, more so than ever. A heart had been harvested. The medical staff came to my bed and placed me upon the trolley to take me into surgery. And so, I went in, to meet a heart. My heart.

CHAPTER 2

A GILDED
CHILDHOOD

What good is every material possession in the world if you don't have your health? It is a question Bhanu was confronted with as I lay in Columbia Medical Center waiting for my heart, but it is an issue I have been aware of throughout my entire life. My brother Rajiv and I were born into a wealthy and prosperous family, with every advantage to speak of when we were growing up, but right from the start there was an awareness that everything could be lost in an instant and that nothing can ever really prepare you for the vicissitudes of fortune. Material comfort may provide a cushion but health is everything and that can be snatched away in the blink of an eye.

This first hit home when we lost our father very early on. He was killed in a car crash when I was just four years old, a dreadful blow to all of us, but we lived with our mother in the warmth of an extended family and on a material level wanted for nothing. On a personal level, too, I was content: I was extremely close both to my mother and Rajiv, a closeness that continued into adulthood and throughout our lives. We grew up as fatherless boys and came to depend upon each other, possibly because when I was still very young, although I was healthy in most respects, a strange set of accidents and ailments took their toll. Why did they happen to me? I can't say. But they did and I have been dealing with the problems and their repercussions ever since those early days.

Throughout my life there have been dramas that have ended up in the Casualty ward – some self-inflicted, others the result either of a freak accident or my innate physical condition, problems that began to surface very early in my life and provided a sharp counterpoint to the otherwise fortunate circumstances in which I lived. They didn't exactly prepare me for the trauma of my heart transplant, which would one day cause such a crisis for my family and me, nor were all these issues in any way a run-up to it, but they did mean that I was no stranger either to dramatic incident or to the doctor's anxious consultation. But the first major incident and my first experience of hospitalisation was entirely my own fault.

The first of these traumas happened when I was eight

years old and the family was preparing to take a holiday to escape the heat of Delhi in the summer. We played a lot of sport outside, burning off the energy of childhood, two little boys running and whooping, carefree, the world our own to enjoy, with the adults clucking affectionately over us, but allowing us the freedom to play and explore, memories that still make me happy thinking about them today. Rajiv and I were always together, the bond we'd had from the very start growing ever stronger, as we discovered the world together, never with a sense of foreboding that one day this might end. Although we had lost our father, death is almost incomprehensible to a child, and accidents are confined to scraped knees and hurt pride. When you are a child, the summer is endless, the range of possibilities is infinite. Except the possibility of tragedy, of course. That never occurs to you.

What happened to me back then was not a tragedy but it was an early indication that life does not always go in order to plan. It certainly didn't on this occasion. I was rather a naughty child and, as on so many other occasions, I was misbehaving. We had gone out on an expedition and I was playing with my fishing hooks. I was practising what I was going to do when we got to the river and so I flicked my rod back and made as if to cast out. As I did so I managed to hook my own finger. The hook went in so deeply that it got caught under the skin. I wiggled it and it went in deeper. I tried to manoeuvre it and it went deeper still, by this time hooking its way through my entire finger, not the bait I had wanted on the end of my fish hook. And on top of everything else, it hurt. This was not how I had been planning to spend my summer at all.

After some moments wrestling with this fish hook, it became increasingly obvious that I would need help. There was nothing for it but to own up to the adults and so, rather reluctantly, I sought out my mother, uncle and aunts. They clustered around, tutting. Various attempts were made to dislodge the hook, but by now it was so firmly wedged into my finger that nothing could be done. A doctor was going to be necessary and so one was duly called.

In the end, not even the doctor could help me, or at least, not until I was taken to a hospital. The hook had gone into my finger so deeply that removing it required a full-scale operation, and any residual annoyance the adults might have felt had by this time turned to a deep concern. And so, for the first of many, many times, I was taken into surgery and underwent a full operation performed under a general anaesthetic. I was put to sleep, but upon coming round some time later, I became drowsily aware that although there was a burning pain in my finger where the fish hook had been, it was out. I soon forgot about it. I was an energetic, healthy little boy and, if anything, the whole experience had actually been rather exciting. I had been in hospital and had had an operation. Who else of my age did I know who could say that? Nor did it put me off fishing. I was soon back out there with my fishing rod to hand. All children have accidents, some major, some minor – it is just a part of growing up and the fish-hook incident can be classed as a salutary lesson on the need to be careful if there's something sharp that can lodge in you. But it was a temporary setback that could be easily repaired.

The same could not be said for what happened next. Not long after that particular incident, my mother decided to take out an insurance policy on me and for that you needed a medical, which was to be performed by the insurance company's doctor. No one thought anything of it: it was a totally standard procedure, which was expected to be little more than a formality. In actual fact, this was the start of a far greater drama in my life, which is continuing to this day.

On the day in question, I was ushered into the doctor's surgery and he started taking my blood pressure, checking out my general health and then produced a stethoscope, which he placed over my heart. This should have been over in a moment, but it wasn't. He took the stethoscope away from me, looked at it and then started listening to my chest again. I was aware of a slight change in his expression: this was not going according to plan. He listened once more and this time there could be no doubting it: 'This chap has a missing beat in his heart,' he told my mother. None of us could have possibly expected this. My mother looked to be in a state of shock.

The doctor did his best to calm us down but it was immediately clear that this was not to be the end of it – further medical advice was needed, not least because at this stage it was not clear exactly what was wrong. He advised us that it was essential to undertake further medical investigations to probe further, although at this early stage it was also not yet clear who would be the best person to see. My mother was a resilient woman, bringing up her children as a single mother, albeit one in the bosom of a very supportive family, but as this came only a few years after the death of my father, it was a dreadful blow to her. In the initial confusion all manner of worst-case scenarios flitted across her mind – how could they not? – but ultimately she was a pragmatic woman and started to work out the best course of action to pursue.

I knew something was wrong, of course, but I didn't know what. As a child it is very difficult to take on board the concept of serious illness and I didn't feel that anything was wrong with me – I felt perfectly normal and continued onwards as before, blithely unaware that something potentially very serious had been discovered, although we did not yet know exactly what was amiss. Every child believes themselves to be immortal and I was no different, no matter what the doctor might have said, and so I continued as I always had done, getting up to mischief with Rajiv and going my own merry way.

But around me, my aunts and uncles began to talk to one another about what they should do next and my mother began to turn to members of our immediate family for help and advice. It was readily forthcoming. As luck would have it, her sister, Krishna Mehra, was married to a medical man called Dr Ram Lal Mehra, who was the Chief Medical Superintendent of the All India Medical Institute of Sciences in New Delhi, a recently established centre of excellence, founded in 1956 by Jawaharlal Nehru, the first Prime Minister of India. After some worried consultation, I was taken to be checked out by Dr K. L. Wig, who was the Director of the Institute and First Dean of the Faculty, but I still remained unaware of the potential seriousness of what was taking place. If anything, I was a little bored by it all and saw the whole scenario as a task assigned by the grown-ups, something that kept me from the far more enjoyable pastime of play.

This was the start of another recurring theme in my life. I have met and been treated by some of the greatest specialists in their field and the first of these was Dr Wig, whose family, like mine, originated in Lahore and settled in modern-day India after Partition. He went on to become one of the founding fellows of the Institute, and, later, the

K. L. Wig Center for Medical Excellence and Technology was named after him. But I was still just a child and didn't realise I was being examined by one of the most esteemed doctors in India at the time. The adults in my family did, however, and so knew that if anyone could sort out the problem and give them the right advice, it was him, which was some consolation to my mother, at least.

And so, the battery of tests began, incomprehensible to a little chap of my age, but the problem was established: my heart had a leaky valve. This meant nothing to me but, naturally, my mother and uncles and aunts realised the gravity of the situation, and also that there was nothing they could do. I was only nine and there was no real incentive to perform surgery on children back then. In fact, we were fortunate that the problem had even been diagnosed at all: the Institute was radically different from anything that had previously existed in Delhi, one of the many examples of Nehru's determination to establish India as a thriving, modern democracy, and certainly providing a standard of medical care that had not existed before. But heart surgery at that stage was a pipe dream, a complete impossibility, and the problem, for now at least, was one that was unable to be resolved.

It goes without saying that my poor mother was frantic with worry. It had been a troubled few years: first she lost her husband, then her younger son had landed in hospital due to a self-inflicted injury, but now there was something far worse – the first intimations of heart disease. I might have been too young to understand the full implications of what had come to light but my mother certainly wasn't and had to confront all the fears that a parent most dreads – that something might happen to her younger child.

But Dr Wig was sanguine and his wise words and counsel worked very well to calm everyone down. 'Don't worry,' he said. 'The boy is only nine years old and nothing will happen yet. In twenty or thirty years' time the situation will have changed and they will be able to do something to help.' At that point, 20 or 30 years to me seemed like an eternity away – an unimaginable amount of time to a small boy – but my mother understood that by the time this leaky valve began to cause real problems, then the technology would exist to treat it.

I didn't understand the gravity of the problem: I was too young. And in any case it didn't have a physical effect on me: I felt perfectly well and could run about and play with Rajiv and all our friends. The fact that, quite literally, at the very heart of me something was wrong, didn't affect me on a day-to-day level at all. And so life continued as it always had done: I didn't exactly forget that my heart would one day need attention but neither did I dwell on it. It was like knowing the earth is round: it's a fact but it has no bearing on one's actual life.

My cousin Sumant and I have been close throughout our lives, not least because in his teens he lived in the Choudhrie-family residence for three years. He also remembers that we were told the problem could be resolved one day. 'You see, you had a congenital heart defect,' he recalls. 'It didn't really affect you on a day-to-day basis because there were no restrictions on the way you were able to behave. These days of course this kind of problem is fairly routine stuff but in those days open-heart surgery was extremely hazardous and it wasn't carried out in India at all.'

The next issue after this came when I was about twelve and wearing glasses, as I always did, and this did have a huge and immediate impact on me. I was the class hockey captain and a group of us were playing hockey at my home one day when one of my fellow pupils swung his hockey stick back and it shattered my glasses and my right eye. I collapsed and doctors were summoned immediately: the right eye was bleeding profusely and I was in terrible pain. To begin with it was unclear how bad the damage was but it quickly became evident that it was catastrophic. While I didn't lose sight in it all together, the damage was such that I would never have proper vision in that eye again.

I was shattered and for a time was plunged into despair. The loss of sight at any age is devastating and as a child all the more so: no longer was I going to be able to play in the carefree way I once had and for a while it seemed that this would have a negative impact upon my education, too. I was in the seventh grade at this point but I had been too badly injured to go back to school. I had to have several operations and I was then taken to London to meet another medical specialist, this time the Harley Street surgeon Sir Stewart Duke-Elder. My mother was as supportive as she could be and helped me in every way imaginable to get through this, but of course, she, too, was shattered. She already knew her younger son had a weak heart and now his vision seemed in danger, too. Her resilience was tested to the core but, as ever, the family rallied round, insisting we see the best experts in the field and did everything they could to improve a very difficult situation.

Again, we were able to see one of the world experts in his area. Sir Stewart was a very famous Scottish ophthalmologist, who dominated his field for decades; he was the author of many highly acclaimed and important books, including seven volumes of *Textbook of Ophthalmology* and fifteen volumes of *System of Ophthalmology*. Like his predecessor, Dr Wig, Sir Stewart said there was a limited amount that they could do at the time, but again like Dr Wig, he was very reassuring and predicted that one day the treatment I needed would be available, even if that were not yet the case. 'He has a good left eye,' he told my mother. 'He will be okay and able to see out of it now, and one day they will develop a way to bring his right eye back.' In the event other problems were to overtake this one.

But although the long-term prognosis was a good one, I didn't cope very well. I was twelve, an age when children want to be running around and discovering the world and instead I was in some ways taken away from it. Initially I went back to school – I was attending St Columbus School in New Delhi, a Catholic institution; and although I am Hindu I can to this day recite the Lord's Prayer – but it was soon obvious that the strain was going to be too great and so I was taken out of school altogether. From then on I was educated privately. One unexpected consequence of studying privately was that I passed my school leaving exams two years earlier than I would have done so otherwise. So by the time my friends joined college, I was already in the third year, which was quite amusing. But nothing else was funny about that episode.

In all it was a very difficult and traumatic time with seemingly endless repercussions. Nor did I start making a recovery: matters actually got worse for a while. I developed double vision and I had to wear spectacles with tinted glass to help me overcome this, but the mind is a great thing and it helped me to be able to see properly once more. After a time my mind automatically removed the second image of my double vision and I was able to see straight again, a situation that exists to this day. I don't think about my double vision at all these days, although it's still present.

Meanwhile people continued to rally around, not just inside my family but outside it too. My tutors were helpful: they were decent, responsible people and they made life easier for me by emphasising that the future was still a bright one. Up until then I had always imagined that I would do well in life, but I was so shattered by what had happened that I began to harbour doubts that I would be able to achieve what I wanted to. However, my teachers helped me to see that nothing had changed and that I would still be able to go on and have the life I had always wanted. Rajiv of course was a great support – although he had initially been extremely scared on my behalf – and as I have always had a fundamentally positive attitude I learned how to cope.

Again, Sumant remembers this crisis. 'You had a lot of support from your mother, so you coped very well,' he reminds me. 'But eye surgery in those days was not what it is now, so you ended up with limited sight in that eye. But you were so positive: although I know you must have been down, I really don't remember you being depressed or inhibited by these problems. But I do remember that the eye stabilised soon afterwards and that while you might not have had full vision you were able to function totally normally. You clearly got used to it.'

My next serious health problem came about a couple

of years later when I was in my teens. I had had a Chinese meal with my family and friends and afterwards I went to indulge in a game of billiards. Quite suddenly, I stopped being able to breathe. I ran outside into the garden, and started to choke, gasping for air, as blackness seemed to swell up around me and I collapsed into it.

I was barely conscious and had no idea what had happened, but I was fighting to breathe. It wasn't related to my heart, I was pretty sure about that, but what could possibly have caused such a violent implosion? Meanwhile there was chaos going on around me, with people shouting for help and trying to resuscitate me. Others stood around helplessly, unable to understand what had gone so badly wrong. My mother was sitting nearby with her brother and sister-in-law drinking tea when it happened; she watched, horrified, as the bystanders began to realise that the person who had collapsed was her son.

Very fortunately my maternal uncle Dr Balrag Krishan Kapur was present. The second of four brothers on my mother's side, he was a doctor in the Army. He realised I was having an extreme allergic reaction of some sort. 'Drink this,' he commanded, pressing a cup of black coffee towards me. I managed to get that cup down, then another and then another. The stimulant from the caffeine gradually began to work. I started to breathe more normally as I drank yet more coffee and we all began to calm down. But the incident, which seemed inexplicable at the time, left me badly shaken, while my poor mother had to cope with yet another shock courtesy of the seemingly endless number of incidents affecting her younger son. Rajiv was terribly concerned, too. And indeed, it had been more serious than I realised at the time.

It was only some time later that an explanation emerged. It turned out that I was allergic to iodine, which is found in seafood, and which I had been eating at lunch that day. Now of course I never go near seafood but this iodine allergy was to cause significant problems some years down the line. Back then, though, I was simply relieved that my uncle had understood the nature of the problem and been so quick to act – and indeed from then on there would be a period of calm for my health that would last some decades. Rajiv and I were now turning our minds to business, creating a company that would one day become a global empire, and for the time being all my energies were to go into that. But of course, at the heart of it all, my heart was a little ticking time bomb, functioning for now, but always threatening to explode and bring devastation in its wake. That is what it ultimately did, of course. But I was to have a respite from all these worries for now, as were my mother and brother, because these ailments hurt not only the people they directly affect, but also the people around them. And so it would prove a couple of decades hence.

CHAPTER 3

BROTHERHOOD

I f you have all the comforts life can offer, what does any of it matter if you lose the people you love? The one constant in my life until his death in 1998 was my brother Rajiv. He was just over two years old when I came along, but throughout our lives we were more like twins than brothers, a closeness strengthened by the fact that we lost our father when we were so young and so we developed an extraordinarily close bond that permeated every facet of our existence. We were children together, men together, celebrated together when times were good and stood shoulder to shoulder when times were bad. We founded our company together and built an empire together. Both as a child and an adult, Rajiv never did anything without consulting me first and his loss is something that has been harder to bear than anything else. I am writing this more than seventeen years after his death and yet it is the one ache in my heart – my new heart as well as my old heart – that will never go away. A heart can break physically, as mine did, but it can also break emotionally, as mine also did, and the pain of the second can be even worse than the pain of the first. However much success I am able to achieve, how will anything ever make up for that?

Rajiv and I grew up very closely together, from a family that originated in the Punjab, where my great-grandfather owned five or six villages, a wealthy man. But that was not the source of my family's growing prosperity. My paternal grandparents came to Delhi in the 1920s after my grandfather, Rai Sahab Banarsi Das Choudhrie, had a vicious row with his father, my great-grandfather, and the first night my grandparents were in the city they slept under a tree along with my father – then a young boy – a marked contrast to the style in which they would later live. But my grandfather had the wherewithal to set up on his own, because his own grandfather had left him 1,000 rupees, which at the time was a king's ransom and enough to allow him to plan for a very comfortable and successful future. To put this in context, at that time you could rent a house for 30 rupees a month. My grandfather did exactly that: he rented a house and started a catering and real-estate business, which expanded rapidly and was the basis of a business empire that made my grandfather a very wealthy man.

My maternal grandfather was also an extremely distinguished personality. My mother's father had been educated in the UK to get a degree as a doctor, but when he returned to Lahore he started to invest in real estate as well as being board director for the Punjab Bank for forty-eight years. He ended up as its chairman, a position he held for sixteen years and finally died at the ripe old age of ninety-six.

My father Shanti Prasad Choudhrie was born in Delhi and educated at St Stephen's College; he married my mother Amrit when he was twenty-three in an arranged marriage, as was the custom in those days. My brother Rajiv was born in 1946 and I followed two years later in 1948. Our bond was instant and immediate. The jealousy that an older child sometimes feels for the new arrival was non-existent: instead, the complete opposite was in its place, the sort of care and concern that is perhaps more to be found in a parent and a child than two brothers. Rajiv, simply, did everything for me. My mother remembers that when I was still a baby and would not stop crying, Rajiv took a sweet out of his own mouth and popped it into mine in an attempt to cheer me up. That could be a metaphor for our entire relationship. Rajiv never really stopped giving me sweets, although not necessarily of the candy variety, as he was always the first person I would turn to when problems arose – and the reverse was also true. We developed a spiritual bond that simply grew and intensified as we matured. As children, we worked together, played together, spoke the same language, had our own in-jokes and rituals and slept in the same room, as close as two brothers possibly could be.

My father was doing very well for himself: based in Calcutta, he was running an auction house for goods confiscated by the courts and employing his own brother-in-law in the process, another family example of two relatives who were close and worked side-by-side. My uncle had two daughters and so the four of us were essentially brought up as brothers and sisters but, in 1953, when I was four and a half, disaster struck. Our hitherto comfortable life together was completely shattered and the first major trauma of my life occurred. It was certainly a lesson that catastrophe can strike out of the blue, just when it is least expected, to devastating effect. My father had been travelling on business when he was killed in a car accident, leaving my mother distraught, a single mother with two very small boys to look after. This was the first of a series of personal tragedies to affect my mother. A stalwart woman, she coped, as she did after the death of Rajiv, by never mentioning what had happened again. She never spoke my father's name. But her grief was a deep one and, in the event, she never married again.

I have no recollection of my father at all, although I must have been very hard hit at the time. Partly this is no doubt because I was only four and a half, an age before memories properly set in, but partly also it may have been down to a sense of self-preservation. If I blocked something very painful out, then subconsciously perhaps I was trying to deal with the grief. This might also have been the reason behind my mother's reticence. But the brain, and memory, contain mysteries of their own and something of that time must have stayed with me because decades later, in the wake of my heart transplant, a clear memory emerged that was rooted in the time just before my father's death, which suggests the impact on me was, unsurprisingly, enormous. But we will return to that episode later.

The entire family was shattered by the accident: it was not just that my mother had lost her husband, but my grandparents had lost their much-loved son. On the one hand, they had to deal with their grief but, on the other, the immediate concern was what would happen to my mother and her two boys, which would have been in keeping with familial traditions in India, where the husband's family is expected to take care of the wife. Ultimately the decision was made that we would return to Delhi to live with my paternal grandparents in their palatial family home and so, despite the traumatic reason behind the move, there began a phase of childhood that was in many ways idyllic, in luxurious surroundings and everything a child could possibly want.

My grandparents' house was a beautiful place to grow up and unusual for Delhi: it was a mansion surrounded by grounds where we had cattle grazing and horses to ride. And although the adults had clearly been scarred by the calamity, Rajiv and I were both still so young that any residual memories of the tragedy that befell my father soon left us and we grew closer still as we started to attend school. In our free time we ran around and explored our new city, settling down to our new life. A new city is a new adventure, especially for two little boys with a new world to discover. Rajiv, as the older brother, was always the more sensible and contained of the two of us; I, the younger brother, could be extremely mischievous and was constantly getting into hot water – from which, equally constantly, Rajiv helped me get out.

The family made it as easy for us as they could. My grandfather Rai Sahaib Banarsi Das was an extremely generous man and we wanted for nothing. He tended to indulge us two boys particularly, perhaps because we'd lost our father and he was trying to make up for that, and provided some quite magical moments in my childhood that have always stayed with me. When I was about five or six years old, my grandfather came home one day with a pair of tiger cubs for us to play with. These beautiful exotic animals lived with us for a while, although when they started to grow they had to go and live in the zoo. We loved them. We were so indulged by my grandfather that other members of the family sometimes asked us to put in a good word when they needed something of their own: when my uncle was going to college, he wanted to have a scooter and asked us to put in a request for him. We did so and a scooter duly appeared.

My paternal grandmother, Suhagwati Devi Choudhrie, was also still with us when I was a small child, and played an active role in family life, getting us ready in the morning, putting us on the school bus, bringing us home for lunch. She was another warm and maternal presence and, like my grandfather, provided help and support for my grieving mother in a practical sense. They could not bring my father back but they could do everything possible to help my mother to cope and to make sure we boys had the best possible start in life. She died when I was about nine, although that is another death I cannot recall happening at the time. My grandfather was to follow her some years later, in 1963, by which time Rajiv and I were in our teens and by which time also my own health complications had begun.

It was a wonderful time to be a young boy: Delhi in

the 1950s saw a time of enormous change and excitement within the country. India had gained her independence one year before I was born: in 1947 she became a republic under our first prime minister, Jawaharlal Nehru, and the sense of emancipation and freedom was palpable, with India in charge of her own destiny, free at last of colonial binds. But it was also a time during which matters sometimes seemed to run out of control: Independence also signalled Partition and the creation of Pakistan – which is where my family originally came from – with all the horror and bloodshed that that entailed.

But there was all to play for. It was to be decades before India turned into the economic powerhouse it is today, but it was still a time of excitement and change with the kinds of opportunities we had never seen before and was the ideal backdrop for two young men determined to make their mark, as Rajiv and I were. Within a decade we would be running our own business and within two decades that business would become a corporate empire with global outreach.

If the child is the father of the man, then that is certainly true in my case, because even as a child I was to start showing the characteristics that played a major role in my life as an adult. For a start, I was always interested in collecting cars: it's just that when I was still very young my collection was of Dinky cars, eventually over one hundred of them. That deep love of cars endured in me – in later years, I was to build up a superb collection of vintage motors, which I now keep in Delhi, and which is one of the greatest passions of my adult life.

Another early interest that foreshadowed a later preoccupation was art. I loved painting and drawing and was pretty good at it, taking part in school and national competitions; decades later, when I became a grandfather, I was able to share this love with my grandchildren, teaching them when they were very young how to draw. And this love of art was to grow: as adults, Anita and I meticulously collected great art, which we keep in our various houses in the UK and India, in particular forging a close bond with the artist known as the 'Indian Picasso', namely M.F. Husain. But while I was still a budding businessman and collector, I had also been an extremely naughty little boy – far more so than Rajiv – constantly playing pranks on my long-suffering family, joking and laughing and larking around. My teachers were sometimes exasperated but I was also – like Rajiv – showing a growing aptitude for dealing with numbers, something that both of us were going to put to very good use once the serious business of building up the company had begun.

The one thing that marred all this, apart from the health problems and accidents that I have already mentioned, was that shortly after my eye injury, I started to have migraine headaches, something that plagued me into adulthood, although it lessened as I got older and finally cleared up all together when I was in my fifties. These headaches were extremely unpleasant: my vision would become blurred, my heart would start pounding and the pain in my head was such that I couldn't bear to see the light. My mother would put me in a darkened room and give me painkillers but relief was slow to come. No one was ever able to establish an actual cause for them, but they were difficult to deal with, another of the health problems that have plagued me throughout my life.

After my grandfather died, the property was split into three and divided between my mother and two uncles, allowing us to continue our very privileged existence and to live in the style we always had done. But we were brought up to understand our obligations, too, and it was impressed upon us from an early age that if you are fortunate then you should give back. My mother was always involved in all sorts of charities: she essentially adopted two young girls, made sure they were brought up properly and secured good marriages for them – both married police officers. They used to refer to Rajiv and me as their younger brothers and we would all tease each other, make jokes and lark around.

There were plenty of other charitable works, too, some involving our religion. In a Hindu home, once a year you must give food to those who are less fortunate and we would all participate in this. People would come from 11am and members of the family would serve the food throughout the day. Every holiday, and on the anniversary of our father's death, our mother would also take us to the Temple, where she would teach us prayers and chanting. Perhaps affected by my eye accident, she donated a lot of money to a local blind school and got involved in the institute's work.

Forefathers of my mother's family had also done many charitable deeds. Her own father had built a school that offered free tuition to students who couldn't pay and they also provided free dentistry and medical help to their local community, as well as donating 150 prosthetic limbs a year. This sense of obligation has stayed with me throughout my life and as an adult I have done as much as I could through charitable giving, to ensure that other people would benefit from, for example, medical research, something I will talk about later in the book.

Rajiv and I were both sporty growing up and, after an education at St Columbus, I went on to college in 1966 at the age of seventeen to study economics. I was a member of the Union and the Principal of the college was constantly on the phone to my family, complaining that I was causing trouble of some sort. I didn't always endear myself to my tutors, either. On one occasion our professor asked us to write a budget on what we would do when running a business after we left college and the class was in uproar when my proposal was read out: I proposed taking a supply company's transport, their buses, turning them into rooms and parking them in the middle of prime real estate and charging for occupancy. Perhaps it is no surprise that I ended up – amongst much else – owning hotels.

I graduated college after three years and went to work on the farm Rajiv and I had bought, an organisation that utilised fully mechanised wheat-seed farming. India was undergoing a series of food shortages at the time, so these new farming methods were creating quite a stir. I used to go to the farm early, at about 6am, work until 10 or 11 and then go home for lunch. In the afternoons I studied astrology and in the evenings I'd go out with my friends. Every Tuesday, I went to a temple dedicated to Hanuman, the Hindu monkey god: I have a very strong spiritual side and believe in reincarnation and destiny – of which more later in the book.

In 1969, Rajiv set up a business for film distribution, which I was part of while still in college before leaving to work on the farm. Then in 1972, Rajiv and I founded an export/import business selling transmitters. We founded this business completely off our own backs: although there was plenty of family money we didn't use it, starting off with a capitalisation of 5,000 rupees, which in today's money is about £50. We started the business just at the moment we could take advantage of the changing times, because although central-government economic controls were still very much in place and would remain so until the early 1990s, new opportunities were opening up all the time. Television had started broadcasting in India in 1959, but remained very limited for many years. In 1972, however, the service was extended to Bombay and Amritsar and more households began to experiment with this exciting new toy. Our business grew rapidly – in 1974, we expanded our exports to Russia and in the early 1980s, the company was awarded the President's Export Award. It was a growing company – any spare resources went into real estate and assets; it was a very exciting time.

Travelling in Russia in the 1980s was an education in itself. This was still the Communist era, and the country was still one in which consumer goods were all but unobtainable except for the privileged elite, the concept of Western-style supermarkets was unheard of and the shops that sold food would have limited goods and customers who would have to queue for hours just to buy a loaf of bread. It wasn't exactly a Shangri-La for the visitor and nothing like travelling in the West. During the weeks, we'd be working, but during the weekends we'd have nothing to do. So we'd often follow the example of the locals and join one of the numerous queues that existed absolutely everywhere, usually without having a clue what we were queuing for. When we got to the front of the queue we'd find out what they were selling and on one occasion it turned out to be bananas. There were four of us at the time and we were only allowed to buy one banana each, so we did exactly that, gave them to the locals and then rejoined the queue at the end to wait until we were allowed to buy the next banana.

On another occasion they were selling biscuits with ice cream in the middle: this time round we were allowed to buy two, so we all did so, ate both of them and then started queuing again. These queues could be crowded and bad-tempered – if you had to use them for food on a regular basis they wouldn't have been much fun – and on one occasion when I was there with my brother-in-law Satish, he was forced to ask the translator to tell one lady to stop pushing him. 'I'm not pushing, I'm breathing!' she snapped.

Of course the hotels were all bugged. Once, to test this out, I commented to one of my colleagues that in India, in business meetings, you are supplied with food, biscuits and chocolate – a choice of beverages – but in Russia you were given black coffee with not even a jug of milk to go with it. I was proved right. The next day when we went into a meeting, the table was groaning under the weight of all the milk, biscuits and chocolate you could imagine, no doubt a surprise to the people who were used to getting food by standing in a very long queue.

By this time I was happily settled down and had started a family. I met Anita in 1973 after I had started to do a little matchmaking myself. I had a friend from college who, like me, had the nickname 'Bunny'. One day I took my then-girlfriend home and went into the house to have a Coke, when her pretty younger sister walked in. I rang my friend. 'Bunny,' I said, 'I have found the girl for you.' I arranged the introduction, which worked spectacularly well as they are now married, and this girl told me she had a friend she thought I should meet. That friend was Anita.

The first date Anita and I went on was at a bowling alley: she beat me, as it happens, which is when I decided she was definitely the girl for me. We dated for a couple of years until, in 1975, we knew we wanted to be married and so I spoke to my mother. Social mores in Indian society were changing and there was no longer the assumption that anyone would have an arranged marriage, on top of which my mother was never hidebound by tradition. Even so, parental approval was, if not crucial, at the very least highly desirable and of course that applied to Anita's parents as well. But both sets of families were accommodating and we were to be married in November 1975, when Anita was in her final year in college. In the event my uncle passed away and the marriage was postponed to February 1976. Our two sons Bhanu and Dhairya were born in, respectively, 1978 and 1982. Meanwhile, Rajiv had married in 1973, with a son Dhruv appearing the following year, and daughter Simran in 1978. Because of the proximity in age the cousins have always been very close.

And so our lives continued. The early years building up the company were great fun: Rajiv and I travelled the world, as I still do, working closely together, supporting one another at work and in private. We were both very good at discussing figures and could move from analysing one division of the company to a totally different one in an instant, and success built upon success. But material wealth and success cannot hold back the vicissitudes of fate and all the success in the world could not, ultimately, save Rajiv. Nor could it protect me because although my heart transplant was the ultimate and most serious of my problems, for some reason, just as in childhood, I continued to have serious health problems that cropped up throughout my life. They were all devastating in their particular ways, but the next crisis threatened to have the most terrible consequences. It now appeared that I was going to lose my sight completely.

CHAPTER 4

I HAD FORGOTTEN HOW BEAUTIFUL ANITA IS

L ife had been very good in the 1980s as Rajiv and I built up the company and we both nurtured our growing families but, in 1990, I encountered a full-blown crisis, the first of the really serious health problems I was to encounter as an adult. Darkness fell, both physically and emotionally. Yet again I was to learn that all the privilege in the world counts for nothing when deprived of a basic part of our existence that we take for granted. I had to cope with the loss of my sight – and for a while it seemed that it would be permanent. Of all the five senses, sight is the one that we perhaps fear losing most because it defines so much of what we can do. Of course there are remarkable people who have been blind from birth or who developed blindness at a later stage and still went on to lead successful and fulfilling lives, but it is a frightening prospect to contemplate never being able to see properly – or at all – again.

As with the repeated breakdowns of my heart, so I was also to suffer more than one breakdown with my sight. My right eye had been damaged since childhood from that accident with a hockey stick so it seemed a particularly cruel irony that my left eye began to fail as well, for totally unrelated reasons, but ones which drove me, uncharacteristically, to near despair. It was only through my contacts in Moscow that I was able to find a quite brilliant surgeon – then totally unknown in the West – who ensured that my eyesight eventually recovered. It was a dreadful ordeal, although in some ways it prepared me for the time when my heart followed suit and threatened to let me down for good.

Sight is one of the most fundamental and crucially important aspects of our lives, but it is easy to take it for granted until something happens to take it away. And because my damaged right eye had learned to cope with the problems I had been presented with, I also took my ability to see the world around me, in all its beauty and sometimes horror, as a matter of course. Despite that earlier accident, it had never previously occurred to me that something could go really wrong with my sight. But it did, although when the problems began it took me a little while to realise that something was really wrong.

I had had to cope with migraines throughout my life, entailing blurred vision and searingly painful headaches and so, one morning, when in London on business, I thought little of it when I couldn't read the newspaper. My sight was blurred, but I simply put it down to the migraine and assumed that matters would quickly right themselves. I was right and a couple of hours later I was able to read again. It did not at that point occur to me that something was really wrong.

But it wasn't long before it became clear that this was not one of my usual migraines. I began to realise that this was a problem of an altogether different magnitude. The next morning I was due to return to Delhi and the same thing happened again: I couldn't read the newspaper first thing in the morning, but a couple of hours later my sight had returned. This time, though, it worried me and I began to realise that it might be something more than a migraine, although at that stage I still had no idea that I would end up actually losing my sight. But I sensed it might be serious so, once back in Delhi, I spoke to Anita about it and, as she always did when a crisis in my health materialised, she began to educate herself fast upon the subject, so much so that both my sons claim she has as much medical knowledge as any doctor.

Anita was aware this could be extremely serious, and she was adamant that I saw an eye specialist. We went to see someone locally and I was subjected to a barrage of tests that took about ten days in total, during which time my sight continued to deteriorate so badly that, ultimately, although I could make out vague shapes and sizes, my vision had become so bad that I was unable to recognise my own wife. While I wouldn't say that panic set in, depression did, for the verdict at the end of this barrage of tests was blunt.

'The central vision in your left eye is gone,' I was told. The problem was macular degeneration and, although I had some slight peripheral vision, it was very weak indeed and I needed help to be guided around and to do the most normal day-to-day things. My family was as supportive as usual, although Rajiv and my mother Amrit could also not conceal their great concern that this problem was never going to be put right. And of course, given that the vision in my right eye had been damaged since my childhood accident, this was absolutely devastating news. The world, quite literally, turned black. I am a very positive person but there seemed little that was positive about this, and as with the other health crises in my life, I was not the only one affected. Anita, always devoted, always loving, was faced with the prospect of the man she had married going blind. Amrit and Rajiv had already suffered on my behalf, undergoing all the pain that a mother and brother feel when seeing the misery of a much-loved family member, and my mother must have wondered why so much seemed to be happening to her younger son. There was no sweet this time that Rajiv could give me to assuage the anguish I was feeling. Darkness had spread across my own personal land.

Salvation, when it eventually came, could not have stemmed from a more unexpected source. Russia in 1990 (and perhaps even now) was certainly not seen as a centre of medical excellence but, oddly enough, it was in Russia that the problem had first come to light. A year previously I had been in Moscow on business and had been suffering some problems in my vision. A colleague of mine, who was working for the company as the manager in Moscow, recommended that I see a physician, a Dr Svyatoslav Fyodorov. It was an inspired suggestion, although it was going to be a while before I realised quite how much he would help me in managing to restore my sight.

Dr Fyodorov was working at a place he had founded in 1988 – the Fyodorov Eye Microsurgery Complex – which in actual fact became one of the world centres of excellence for the kind of surgery that he practised. Meanwhile, Dr Fyodorov himself, who went on to become involved in Russian politics but very sadly died in a helicopter crash in 2000, came to be considered as the father of refractive surgery, the type of surgery used to improve the refractive state of the eye to decrease or eliminate dependence on glasses or contact lenses. He was the next in a series of world-class surgeons with whom I was to become acquainted and ultimately treated by in my life.

His was an interesting life. Born to Russian parents in what is now Khmelnytskyi, Ukraine, Fyodorov had two artificial legs after losing the original ones from slipping under a tram; this put paid to his desire to become a pilot and he had to choose another career instead. Subsequently graduating from the Rostov Medical Institute in Rostov-on-Don, he went on to practise as an ophthalmologist. In 1960, he invented a cure for cataracts, when he performed the first-ever intraocular lens-replacement operation. In 1973, this immensely gifted man developed another new surgical technique to cure the early stage of glaucoma, following that up with radial keratotomy, which cured myopia by changing the shape of the cornea – another groundbreaking technique that was to help make his name. In 1980, he went on to head the Moscow Research Institute of Eye Microsurgery, before founding his own complex in 1988, and it is to him that I owe my sight.

When I discovered him, the complex was still in its early stages and Dr Fyodorov, while a pioneering surgeon who was to become world-famous, was still barely known outside of Russia, a country then very much shielded by the Iron Curtain, although that would shortly come down. I had visited the USSR many times, but the open communication that existed between India, Europe and the United States was not there and there was no one outside the country I could ask about him. I was uncertain but, in 1989, I decided to go along and hear what he had to say.

It was not good news. He told me that my retina was weak and there was a danger it could break at any time. He suggested a particular course of laser treatment, which he said would ensure that if and when the retina broke, it would do so from the side and not from the centre. This meant that my peripheral vision would be damaged but my central vision would be left intact.

It was a very big decision to make: any kind of surgery carries its own risks and to consider operating on my eye at a time when my vision, while occasionally blurred, was still good seemed a dangerous course of action to take. And so, at the time, after consulting with Anita, I didn't take the doctor up on it, not least because there were other centres of excellence we could visit in the UK or the US. 'You were very reluctant,' a colleague agreed. 'I remember though that you were not like your usual self. There was an air of depression hanging over everyone.'

Dr Fyodorov did make an impression on me, however, and he was clearly a man who knew what he was talking about. Until someone actually loses their sight they cannot imagine the full enormity of it, but I had become worried by now and I wanted at least a second opinion. So Anita and I flew to London to visit the world-famous Moorfields Eye Hospital and asked the doctors there what they made of my Russian doctor's diagnosis. 'It's true that the retina is weak, but to undertake any treatment now is like saying the bones in your leg are weak and so we should put them in plaster,' was the verdict. And because of this advice we did nothing, with the result that I very nearly went blind. Western medicine certainly saved me when my heart eventually failed but, on this particular occasion, it let me down very badly.

Everything happened as Dr Fyodorov predicted. A year later, the crisis came and I lost all but my peripheral vision completely. We returned to Moorfields and I was examined again: the verdict was blunt and it shook me to my very foundations. 'This is a one-in-a-million case,' the doctor said. 'The retina is broken, there is nothing you can do and technically you are blind.' This was utterly dreadful news – coming on top of everything else, it momentarily seemed too much. Anita was devastated but, as always, she was there, organising further doctors' appointments, requesting that we should see more specialists – demanding that something must be done.

And so we embarked on a sort of world tour of eye specialists, each of them more useless than the last. Our next stop was New York. 'Technically, you're blind, young man, so get used to it,' said the doctor there, who might have had a medical degree but certainly hadn't spent any time at charm school. From there we went to San Diego, where I was told that the left eye was beyond repair, but there was a chance they could do something with the right eye – the one that had been damaged in childhood – but that it would take at least four or five operations. And even then of course there was no guarantee of success. We went back to Delhi – I was very downcast and sank into a really deep depression. The darkness of my mood matched the darkness that surrounded me. For a time it seemed that all hope was gone.

While back in Delhi, an odd thing happened: an astrologer visited us and made a prediction. 'You will have to go abroad,' he said. 'There will be minor surgery on the left side of your head and your sight will come back.' At the time, far from offering hope, this seemed ridiculous. I didn't take him seriously and sent him on his way. By now I had seen three specialists, who all said that the situation was hopeless. What could an astrologer know about it? However, as it turned out, he was right.

Just as I was becoming blackly resigned to both heart problems and loss of sight, I sent my medical papers to Dr Fyodorov, who had heard what had happened. 'Come back here and see what can be done,' he said. I thought, I don't have anything to lose, so all of us – Anita, my mother, our two sons and me – packed up and went back to Moscow, to see Dr Fyodorov again. His take on it was completely different from the doctors we had seen in the West. 'It's quite simple,' he said. 'Look on your eye as a field that has been deprived of water. If we suddenly flood the field with water, the chances are the core will survive. So what I'm going to do is cut you here [he indicated my left cheek], stop the water supply into your cheek, increase the blood supply into your eye and your sight will come back.'

Again, I thought, what do I have to lose? No one else had been able to suggest anything positive and the loss of sight in my good eye was extremely traumatic. If the worst came to the worst, I wouldn't be able to see, but I couldn't see anyway so I decided to put my faith in the Russian medical system, or at least into this practitioner of it, and have the work done. I agreed to the procedure and with my family – Anita, my mother and the boys – all in attendance, we were in Moscow to make one last-ditch attempt to save my sight. There was none of the fun that we had previously had on our Moscow trips, none of the queuing to see what we would end up with, and none of the deliberate testing to see whether we were being bugged; rather, it was a sombre atmosphere of resolution. My mood was as black as the darkness surrounding me and, although everyone else was extremely supportive, as usual, I was very much aware that this was to be my last hope.

I arrived at the hospital, still very unconvinced about

what was going to happen and, after preparing for what was quite a minor procedure, the doctor cut a vein in my left cheek, sending the supply of blood instead into my eye, and put a patch over the left eye. Then I went back to the hotel and rested. The world still seemed very black.

The next morning, having been told to remove the patch, I returned to the hospital. As we sat in the traffic, I found myself able to gaze out of the window from the front seat of the car. And it took me a moment to realise what was happening. I shut my eyes, blinked a couple of times and then looked out again – and there it was, I was certain: 'I can read the number plate in front of me,' I said. The car erupted, with everyone screaming. My sight had started to come back.

The sun had come up; there was lightness in my life once more. It was hard to tell if we were laughing or crying. Dr Fyodorov had been true to his word and my only question to myself was: why on earth had I wasted time visiting all these other experts? This wonderful doctor had restored the sight he had previously warned me I would lose a full year ago. No matter, now it was done. The relief and the happiness flooding through me were so great that the fear I had felt so recently about never being able to see again was all but forgotten. The boys were so very young that they could not really have been aware of the severity of the situation, but Anita, Amrit and the boys were as relieved and as happy as I was. Darkness had been banished from the land.

Once back in Delhi, my doctors there literally could not believe that my sight had been restored. The world tour resumed – I returned to the doctors in the UK and the US, and everyone's verdict was the same: that it was a miracle. They all asked the same question: 'How did Doctor Fyodorov do it?' When I relayed that question back to him, he laughed, but he was also pretty blunt in his reply: 'Why should I give them my technology?' Every other medical professional was absolutely flummoxed about what had happened. When I saw one very famous professor at the UCLA, he was non-plussed. 'There is no basis at all that we can understand for the restoration of your sight,' he said. 'All we can say is that this has been a miracle cure.'

Throughout this horrendous time, as I said, as ever, Anita was the rock and support I could depend on totally. Sumant witnessed it all, commenting now, 'When this episode of blindness occurred, Anita nursed him and looked after him totally. I have never really seen this level of devotion from anyone.' He commented that I became very dependent on my wife in a way that I never had been before. Certainly, one by-product of all the health issues – the traumas that have crept up periodically through my life – is that my relationship with my wife has strengthened and deepened.

The biggest traumas still lay ahead but at that point she was there when I couldn't see, made herself an expert on the various procedures I would have to undergo and looked after me as much as it was possible for any woman to do.

Indeed, our whole family grew closer as we pulled together and dedicated ourselves to one another; although, of course, at that stage, both our boys were very young and didn't fully understand what was going on. They were aware, though, that I had lost and then regained my sight, and were wildly excited on my behalf, even if they didn't fully recognise how serious the situation had been, or how very close I had come to being blind for the rest of my life.

About a year later, I returned to the hospital in Moscow for some more laser treatment that would restore my eye to near-perfect vision. I was the first foreigner in Russia ever to receive this treatment. When I got to the hospital, there was something that looked like a production line: Dr Fyodorov became famous for conducting his treatments via an 'assembly line', in which patients on operating tables were rotated between a series of different doctors, who in each case were responsible for one part of the operation. Perhaps the geographical location of the clinic influenced this: Russia was just emerging from decades of communism when the clinic was established and so the assembly line was not an uncommon phenomenon when the clinic was set up. But whatever the reasoning behind it, it worked.

I was there for treatment with a new type of laser that didn't exist anywhere else in the world. The doctors prepared me for this ground-breaking procedure as I – like the other patients on the assembly line – was passed from one doctor to the next. The treatment itself only took about two minutes. The one big drawback was that the pain was horrendous, absolute searing agony, so much so that I was screaming in pain – it actually felt as if the eye was being pulled out of its socket. Afterwards, I was given some painkillers, which somewhat alleviated the agonising throbbing in the eye, and was again told to go and rest. Within twenty-four hours, the pain had subsided and my vision had improved significantly. I underwent a few more sessions of laser treatment and the pain turned out to be completely worth it as I finally regained full vision in the eye, something the doctors in the West had written off as a medical impossibility. In Moscow, I was also told that they would be able to repair some of the damage to my right eye and so my eyesight generally began to improve all round.

Through it all, I began to rediscover everything around me with a sense of wonderment. My eyesight was sharper than it had been since childhood and I began to perceive colours in my surroundings more vividly. And nor was it just a case of being able to read again, either. My relationship with Anita had gone far beyond just the surface level many decades earlier: initial attraction is crucial but it is the depth and shared spirituality of the bond that really makes a difference and that is what ties us together above all. As my vision continued to improve, I was reminded again of quite how stunning the woman is that I am married to. Throughout the period of my blindness, I had forgotten quite how beautiful Anita was. I was never to forget that again.

That wasn't an end to my improving eyesight, either. A few years ago, I had a cataract operation, in which the cataract was removed and a lens was inserted into my eye, with the result that although I had worn glasses all my life, I no longer needed to. And so, as I got older, I ended up with a stronger heart and better eyesight.

I have sometimes wondered if the trauma of losing my sight – and for some time thinking I would never recover from it – was in some way, a forerunner for when I would have to lose – and gain – a heart. Perhaps I learned that I could overcome very severe adversity and that when the world seemed black – quite literally on that occasion – there was always hope. It certainly made me aware, again, that health is fragile, that what you take for granted can be whisked away in an instant. The blinded Duke of Gloucester in *King Lear* comments, 'I stumbled when I saw,' but then, we all do. We might be able to see what is happening around us – but none of us can see what will happen next in life.

CHAPTER 5

A HEART BEGINS TO BREAK

With my sight newly restored, the world had taken on a rosy glow again and life went back to normal, with the constant cycle of work and travel slotting into place once more. The bond between the two of us as strong as ever; Rajiv and I continued to expand the business and we were both having the joy of seeing our families growing up. But right at the heart of my body – indeed, in my heart itself – the imbalances that had been there since my childhood remained. The leaky valve continued to leak and the time was fast approaching when that valve would have to be fixed. It had kept going for as long as it could but it would soon stop functioning properly.

Given that it had been faulty throughout my life, my heart had served me well; by now I was in my late forties and most of my major health scares had been of a different nature – although there had been one nasty episode a few years previously when the treatment, or rather examination to find out what was wrong with me, was briefly worse than the ailment itself. As described earlier, after my childhood experience of practically collapsing after a game of snooker, I knew I was allergic to seafood, but *not* to iodine, which is contained within seafood. There is some debate within the scientific community as to whether people who are allergic to seafood will also be allergic to iodine, and to the full extent of any such link, but I can only say that, in my case, I am very definitely allergic to both, as I was to find out.

This became clear during what should have been a standard procedure to check on the state of my heart, but which turned into the stuff of nightmare. At some point in the late 1980s, some of my doctors decided I should have a coronary angiography, in order to establish the state of my leaky valve. Usually this is a straightforward procedure, whereby a catheter is inserted into a blood vessel in the groin or arm and passed up to the heart and coronary arteries. Contrast medium, which is a type of dye (containing iodine) is injected into the catheter and an X-ray, or angiogram, is taken. The contrast medium shows up on the angiogram, charting the voyage it has taken through the body, and this was indeed carried out to highlight what was happening to my valve. The procedure is carried out under local anaesthetic and normally takes about half an hour.

It is fair to say that, in my case, matters did not go according to plan. It is known that some people can have a very adverse reaction to it, ranging from a mild itching to a life-threatening situation – I came down on the severe end of the scale! As soon as the contrast medium had been injected, my body reacted immediately; just as happened all those years earlier, after eating seafood, I stopped breathing and collapsed. The doctors reacted swiftly: while they might have been panicking internally, fearing that they had inadvertently killed me, they recognised straight away that I was experiencing a severe allergic reaction and immediately gave me a 200mg injection of steroids – a huge amount and not the last time I was to be given that much.

Gradually, panting for breath, shaking and exhausted from the ordeal, I began to come back to myself. But to deal with this issue was an unexpected development – who would have thought that a congenital heart defect would ultimately cause such a severe allergic reaction that it turned into a medical emergency itself? It has remained an issue ever since: these days I have to have a tomography – or CT scan – every few years, in order to keep track of the state of my heart, during which time they have to keep the iodine levels under control with repeated doses of steroids. It is something I'll have to live with for the rest of my life.

But back then, these were future concerns, events still lying ahead. All anyone was worrying about at that moment was getting me back on my feet and back to normal, which the doctors duly did. After a day or so of rest, I was completely back to my usual state. And the test didn't go to waste: once all the drama was over, the doctors were able to tell me that the valve would need to be replaced at some point – but not for now.

What is life without hope? Nothing – and so, in the face of all the evidence that had been presented to me since I was a child, I still hoped that nothing further would come of it. I hoped that my battered old heart would continue to do its best and that not only would I never actually need a heart transplant, but that even the valve would miraculously sort itself out. It was not to be and underneath it all I always knew it was not to be. I just managed to put it out of my mind and never brooded on it. I am a very positive person, always looking for an upside in every situation, but I knew, as I always had done, that the time of reckoning would one day come.

For the best part of a decade, my valve still just about managed to function but this situation could not go on forever. By 1996, my fragile but hardworking heart was literally beginning to break. It was to do so twice over in the coming years, both physically and emotionally, but now the first cracks had started to show. This was a moment that I had known all my life might – almost certainly would – come about, but no matter how much we think we know, none of us can really prepare for the future and what our state of mind will be. This heart, my heart, the heart I was born with, had been pumping the blood around my body for as long as it was able but, by now, hobbling along as it strove to do its duty – the duty every heart has towards the person it inhabits – it was really going to start to need some help.

Dramas do not take long to turn into a crisis and once everything began to break down, it all started to happen quite fast. In mid-1996, I came to London for a stress test, to see how my heart was bearing up. It went well. 'The heart valve is OK, you won't need to do anything for at least five years,' I was told. Thus reassured, I went about my business as before. The only problem was that the doctors were wrong. Just a few months later, in December, when I was still in India, I was felled by a bout of pneumonia, which necessitated a stay in hospital and ended up with my situation going from bad to worse, with a complete crisis in my health occurring and one trauma piling up on the next.

I just couldn't get any better: I was ailing, feverish, feeling terrible, weak and wretched. This wasn't just pneumonia – which in itself can be a killer – it was something more.

'Your fever wouldn't go,' Anita remembers. 'You were getting weaker and frailer and, although no one knew exactly what was wrong, the doctors all thought that it had something to do with your heart.' As it turned out, they were right, although there were problems to surmount before we could start on the heart itself. There were continuing doubts about my health so, just before I left the hospital, on 1 January 1997, the heart specialists in the hospital examined me again. I knew immediately that it wasn't just (just!) pneumonia. Within just a few months of my positive check-up, my situation had deteriorated massively and now we were going to have to act. I had been granted such success in so many areas of my life – but when it came to my health, I had been struck down repeatedly and now the situation was about to become more serious than it ever had been before.

I still believe that this sudden sharp deterioration could have had something to do with my state of mind. By this time, in a horrible coincidence, it had emerged that Rajiv also had serious heart problems and it may well have been that my growing concern for my brother was having a bad impact on my own health. We were both desperately concerned about each other and, paradoxically, that was not having a good effect on our own individual states of health. Certainly, I firmly believe that his death was one of the reasons my own heart finally gave up the ghost and

70

broke, both physically and spiritually, although that was at this point still a couple of years away.

But something had gone really wrong with me now and so, the family alerted, I visited a clinic in London's Harley Street, Anita, as always, by my side. What happened there might be taken as a grim rehearsal of what would happen in the run up to the transplant a couple of years later; as the doctors began their investigations, Anita stayed by my side. Living in some discomfort herself, she sensed that I needed her and was depending on her, not just physically but spiritually, too. And it rapidly emerged that the situation was worse than anyone had thought.

What had initially been thought to be an infection turned out to be paratyphoid, a potentially fatal bacterial infection that is caused by contaminated food and water and is not uncommon in India. This was partly why I would eventually make Europe my home after the transplant itself, when I needed to live in as clean an environment as possible. This obviously complicated matters. While I was ill with paratyphoid, a heart operation was out of the question but, at the same time, I needed that heart operation and the longer we delayed it the worse it was going to be.

The answer was to be pragmatic: clear up the paratyphoid and then take matters from there as far as the heart operation was concerned. Antibiotics helped but my all-round level of health was so weak that I needed to be nursed back to health in every other way as well. Anita takes up the story again: 'They isolated you, but they let me stay with you and sleep on the floor as there were no beds for patients' families,' she remembers. 'We knew now that the valve had to be changed but the operation could not be done when you were so frail. We had to build up your physical strength, which took about a month and a half, and I cooked for you myself, as well as making sure you were taking lots of vitamins.' In essence, I was being made strong enough to be able to undergo a massive shock to the system: my first experience of open-heart surgery, which would take place in New York.

As she did so often when my health reached crisis point, Anita had taken charge, and the important thing now was to find out who was best to do the surgery. Everything was readied as I slowly began to regain my health. When I was able, we flew to the US for an operation that was, ironically, going to knock me flat out again, but my situation was getting increasingly serious and with every delay to the operation, the more serious the situation was set to become.

We settled into a New York hotel, and prepared for the first of my two major heart operations. To add to the list of eminent figures of surgery who had seen me during my life, I would be treated by two people: one was Dr Naresh Trehan, an immensely distinguished Indian cardiovascular and cardiothoracic surgeon, who, since 1991, has served as the personal surgeon to the President of India, and who had been a longstanding doctor of mine back in India; the other was Dr Stephen B. Colvin, a pioneer in the treatment of leaky valves, who performed the actual surgery itself at New York Medical Center. With Dr Aubrey Galloway, Dr Colvin (who died in 2008, aged just sixty-four) had invented the Colvin-Galloway Future Band, in which a malfunctioning mitral valve was not replaced but reconstructed and reshaped with a type of prosthetic ring. It was this procedure which would be used on me.

And so, the operation to mend my leaky valve finally took place, decades after it had first been diagnosed in India. My heart, by now, had expanded, as was to be expected, because it needed to work harder than a completely healthy heart to keep the blood pumping around my body; but I still retained some hope that this valve operation would be enough and that I would avoid the full transplant. The operation lasted for several hours. In the course of it, my heart stopped several times, which meant the doctors had to administer short, sharp electric shocks to get it started again. As I was coming round from the operation, they started to test my pulse rates, at which point my heart failed again, necessitating more shock treatment. This went on for about two hours, before I was taken back to my room to rest.

There followed what can only be described as a near-death experience, in which I seemed to see my life slipping away from me, before my very eyes. Anita was at my side as always and remembers well what happened next: my pulse rate suddenly rose above 200 beats per minute – the normal rate is 60 to 100 and anything over 120 can be dangerous. I didn't realise exactly what was happening but, suddenly, I felt a sharp deterioration in my condition. I called out urgently: 'I'm going!' The nurse rushed over and I could see by her face that something was seriously wrong: she pressed a red-alert button and, in a twist that would have been darkly comic if it hadn't been so serious, it promptly turned out that the lifts had jammed. Even so, this was a place that was equipped to deal with an emergency and, within seconds, a medical team had assembled at my bedside, with all the precision of a military manoeuvre, to fight as hard as any soldier would – but in this case to save, not take, a life.

My initial reaction had been urgent but now everything seemed to slow down. I was already beginning to slip away but I was just aware enough to notice that the medical team pushed my family out – Anita, my mother and Rajiv, who was himself not well at all by that stage – all of them looking distraught. I could just hear Anita gasping, 'It wasn't meant to be like this,' before I began to fade to still. The heart monitor on the nurses' station was now running in a straight line, a sign that my poor, beleaguered heart had now stopped beating altogether. My heart had come to a halt.

Outside, my family were beside themselves. 'We were just holding one another and I kept saying, "It wasn't meant to be like this",' Anita recalls. 'This was not to be my husband's destiny. I was thinking of the children, thinking that my older son was probably on a plane, making his way to the hospital while all this was happening and what would it be like for him to arrive here and discover his father had passed away? How could this be happening after all we had gone through, when he'd just had the treatment that was meant to save his life?' Inside the room, the medical team was fighting harder than ever to ensure she was right.

But I was slipping far away now, barely conscious of anything, with a sense that at any moment I could glide away, free of my body, free of my calamitously damaged heart. There was not even a sense of, 'Is this it?', simply a sense that my heart couldn't take it any more and was finally going to give up fighting a battle that it had never been equipped for, a battle for which it had been deprived of its armour, in the shape of a valve that wasn't up to the job. The line indicating that my heart wasn't beating was still straight. I was completely unconscious now. This was finally to be the end.

Except it wasn't. The doctors and nurses at the New York Medical Center were not about to give up: although

I was now completely unconscious and on my way to a different realm, the medical team were there to save lives and they were sure as anything going to save mine. Over and over again they applied electric shocks to my body, determined to bring me back from the dead and, eventually, I began to respond. My battered heart, with its newly restored valve, began to beat again. Anita was right: it was not my destiny to go at that point. In all it took about half an hour for them to get me fully back into the land of the living, at which point one of the medics went out to reassure my distraught family. "'It's OK,'" Anita says she remembers him telling her, "'he made it back." Somehow I knew there was life after this,' she says now. 'I never really felt it would be the end. The driving point was that I never believed this was your destiny. At the heart of it all, I knew you would be fine.'

I had indeed made it back, but there was still quite a way to go. In some ways recovering from the valve surgery was actually worse than the transplant would be. At least in the latter case I would be on my own or with my family during recovery, but here there were other patients present and their distress as they came round from their own operations was such that it made my own even greater. When I came to, in the recovery room, I could hear other people around me, groaning and crying out. I started to hallucinate, thinking that they were trying to kill me. I was on extremely strong painkillers, among much else, which were opiates, and as such were blurring the lines between fantasy and reality. I could hardly tell what was actually going on around me any more. Bhanu arrived in due course and was very distressed by my condition, little knowing, of course, that two years later he was going to have to go through it all again.

At first the recovery seemed as bad as the condition itself but then matters began to improve. What made a huge difference was when a defibrillator was inserted, after which my recovery really began to gather pace. A defibrillator is often confused with a pacemaker but they are different: a pacemaker is there to keep the heart beating at a proper rate, whereas a defibrillator, which has a pacemaker built into it, is there to shock the heart if there are signs of cardiac arrest, which clearly in my case was a possibility. Subsequently the defibrillator was called on to kick in only once, when my heart slowed down in Monaco; but in the immediate aftermath of the operation, it would benefit me hugely.

I began to feel myself again, with a real sensation that I had been given a new lease of life. I was allowed out of the hospital after many weeks and we went back to our hotel in New York overlooking Central Park: in my comfortable surroundings I began to feel much better and even began to hope that this operation was enough to put a halt to the problems and that perhaps a transplant would not be necessary after all. Alas, I was wrong, but back then such was the relief that it had all gone right, I couldn't worry about the future any more. I was just glad to be alive. What I did worry about, though, was Rajiv, whose health was getting steadily worse. Mine was not the only Choudhrie heart that was not performing as it should.

And although I was feeling better than I had done in months, the medication I had to take came with side effects that quite frequently caused the most terrible problems in themselves. With some serious health issues this can turn into a vicious circle: if you don't get the treatment you will die but, if you do get the treatment, you will end up with some other dreadful problem, which the specialists will also have to treat.

The body can make a full recovery, even if in my case it requires a great deal of medication to function properly, but there are some wounds to the spirit or the soul that can never fully recover. The loss of one of the people you love most in the world is something from which no one can ever really get over. You learn to deal with the pain but it stays with you. What use is all the prosperity in the world, if it couldn't save Rajiv, the beloved brother with whom I had shared my entire life?

CHAPTER 6

MY BROTHER, RAJIV

What can I say about Rajiv? Everybody liked him. He was the life and soul of the party, exuberant, loving life, living it to the full. He was everything to me, my soulmate from the moment I came into this world, the big brother, older by two years, who would do anything for me, comforted me when I was ill or sad, rejoiced with me when times were good. In fact I could say anything and everything about Rajiv: he was the apple of my mother's eye and mine too – never could two brothers have been closer. Sometimes an older child can resent it when a younger one comes along – the opposite was true in our case. I will never really understand why he was taken from us so early. I miss him to this day.

I was a naughty little boy but, as we grew up, friends

and family always said that Rajiv was the extrovert while I was sometimes a little quieter. I was certainly the one who suffered repeated bouts of bad health. From an early age, I knew about my leaky valve, aware it would one day have to be dealt with, and had to cope with other episodes along the way, such as the accident that damaged my eye. Rajiv had none of that. Bursting with good health – unlike me – as an adult he would smoke and drink, looking forward with his boundless energy to the future – a future that was to be cut cruelly short.

Like me, Rajiv was married with children: he and his wife Rita were blessed with their son Dhruv, born in 1974, and daughter Simran, born in 1978, companions to my own children. The business we founded together thrived and my own heart problems were the only blot on what otherwise seemed a very sunny horizon. So we were all extremely shocked when, in 1994, it emerged that Rajiv had heart problems too. It came to light because he contracted the flu and the illness would not go away: it lasted for six months and ultimately hit his heart muscle. My nephew Dhruv also believes it is possible that he had contracted a virus which had lain dormant for many years but contributed to the problem. At any rate, to all our shock he was eventually diagnosed with cardiomyopathy, or chronic disease of the heart muscle.

Initially, Rajiv carried on as if nothing was wrong. None

of us realised exactly how serious the situation was to become, and for now at least he was determined to live life as normal. His illness had no impact on the way he carried on the business and an external observer would have had no idea that anything was wrong.

Rajiv made a great many friends throughout his life, with people who would come to grieve his loss very sadly. One of these relationships was with the noted politician R. K. Dhawan, a member of the Indian Congress Party and an aide to the Gandhi family, especially Mrs Indira Gandhi, who was twice Prime Minister of India before her assassination in 1984. Mr Dhawan remembers now: 'As relations grew between us and the Choudhrie family, you all came to know the Gandhi family and we all became close friends. During Indira Gandhi's difficult time in 1977 to 1980, when she was no longer Prime Minister, the Choudhrie family stood behind her in all possible ways and offered all the help you could, which meant she had a very soft spot for you all.'

After Mrs Gandhi's assassination, when her son took over as Prime Minister, the closeness between our two families prevailed, but at this time with some personal risk to my brother Rajiv. An investigation had been launched into Indira Gandhi's assassination and Mr Dhawan, as one of her closest associates, became caught up in it. 'Some persons who were inimical to me for reasons not to their liking

tried to implicate me in the assassination,' he says quietly,
sitting in his peaceful Delhi home below a photograph
of Mrs Gandhi. [He was subsequently fully and entirely
exonerated.] 'There used to be sentries posted outside
my house and they would monitor the persons coming
to see me, note down their car numbers and later harass
them. Rajiv used to come and see me every morning
during that period. I said to him one day, "Car numbers
are being noted and this may create problems with you."
His immediate reaction was, "Since the family has seven
cars, I'll come every day in a different car so they can note
down those numbers and we'll see if it affects the business."
This shows the character of the Choudhrie family. They
showed absolute commitment, loyalty and integrity and
never tried to exploit their closeness to the Gandhi family.
I would not hesitate to say that there is no one who can
match them.'

Another measure of my brother's strength of character
and the love and loyalty he inspired in the people who
worked for him comes through Arun, who was hired
by Rajiv and the relationship between the two of them
became so strong that it was more akin to a father/son
relationship than that of employer and employee. Speaking
to Arun nearly twenty years after my brother's death, it
is plain that the devotion Arun felt for him has never
dimmed. Normally a very jovial and lively fellow, Arun's

demeanour changes to one of sadness and reflection when he remembers my brother and what he did for him as a young man.

'I met Mr Rajiv Choudhrie when I was going through one of the lowest periods of my life because he was a friend of my aunt,' Arun recalls now. 'I was in my early thirties and not sure what I was going to do, but he gave me the chance, the opportunity to come and work for him. He only knew I had been to the same school that his son Dhruv attended. But such was the generosity of his character that he was prepared to give me a chance, after my personal business venture had collapsed.'

'When I joined the company, your brother already knew he had serious health issues, but I have never seen a person cope in the extraordinary way he did,' Arun remembers. 'At first I wasn't aware of the problems, but gradually I became so, only as I was working so closely with him. He was so positive and so strong that no one would have guessed that he was actually seriously ill. Only his wife Rita knew the full extent of it and what he was going through.

'I cannot say enough about his compassion, patience, passion, leadership and his humanity. He was the most generous man I have ever met. Once, I recall Dhruv having a party at the family farmhouse in Delhi, on a night when the temperature was freezing, and one of the office subordinates was there, underdressed and shivering badly. Mr Rajiv

Choudhrie noticed this, pulled him into the farmhouse, pulled out a very expensive-looking white leather jacket and put it on him, saying, "Wear this now so you're not standing in the chill." On another occasion, I saw him get out of the car at a red light in Delhi and start distributing blankets to the street urchins. He was an exceptionally kind man.' That was my brother all over: the fact that he had a serious illness was never going to stop him being aware of the needs of others and doing what he could to help.

Rajiv loved life and he loved what could make life a lot of fun, too. And so he continued to smoke – although less openly than he had done. The problems really began in 1996 when Rajiv became very unwell and, by 1997, he was experiencing such severe heart failure that it was deemed that he needed a transplant. We had explored the options around the world and it was now apparent that the best place to go for an operation was at a world-famous institution in Spanish Harlem on New York's Manhattan Island, the very same place that was to later play such a major part in my own life. This had become a real crisis and we were all beginning to dread what might happen next. 'I got a call from my mother, saying my father was ill and we'd be flying him out to New York,' remembers my nephew, Rajiv's son, Dhruv. 'It was an awful, scary time.'

Even today, Rajiv's daughter, Simran, also remembers this dreadful period with a good deal of pain, although the family tried to protect her from the full extent of what was going on. 'He was not well at all, but I was just sixteen and they were not telling me everything,' she says, her emotion still evident. 'We went to New York and it became apparent that he needed a heart transplant.'

And so it was Rajiv who first went to Columbia Hospital for a transplant evaluation and his decision to go there was a contributory factor for me when it was time to decide where my own transplant should be done. It was Rajiv who first met Dr Donna Mancini, a feisty native New Yorker of Italian extraction, who battled as hard as she could to save his life, and later did exactly the same for me. Dr Mancini – one of the most important players in the story of my health – is small in stature but a giant in everything else. One of the many internationally acclaimed MDs to have treated me throughout my life, she received her Doctor of Medicine from Albert Einstein College of Medicine at Yeshiva University, before completing her internship and residency at Bronx Municipal Hospital Center and fellowship at the Albert Einstein Medical Center in Philadelphia.

Dr Mancini is now a recognised leader in treating patients with advanced heart failure and has been elected to the American Society in Clinical Investigation in honour of her work. She is also these days the Choudhrie Professor of Medicine at the College of Physicians and Surgeons at

Columbia University and Medical Director of the Center for Advanced Cardiac Care. Her petite exterior belies the superwoman within: Dr Mancini is one of the team of doctors to whom I owe my life.

Sadly, through absolutely no fault of her own, she was not able to save Rajiv. 'Rajiv was suffering from cardiomyopathy,' she says, somewhat subdued, in her small office on the twelfth floor of Columbia Hospital, still dressed in scrubs and clogs during a brief interval in a very hectic schedule. She is very much at the heart of Columbia, one of the team of dedicated experts there who have spent their lives giving others hope and life. 'When he came to Columbia he needed a transplant and I would have gone on fighting to get him on that list and I'm really sorry he didn't come back here.' Ultimately, Rajiv was to end up at another hospital but, unfortunately, although that too was a renowned centre of excellence, the team there was not able to save him either.

Rajiv's condition briefly improved to such an extent that he was able to fly back to Delhi and for a short time we hoped all would be well. But then in 1998, his condition deteriorated sharply and this time there was no doubting that he needed treatment – and fast. Although neither of them knew it at the time, this would mark Rajiv's farewell to India.

'I got a call from a renowned cardiologist called Dr McKenna, who was treating him and he said he was not doing at all well,' Dr Mancini recalls. 'I really wanted him to come back here to Columbia but he decided to go to the Cleveland Clinic instead.' Rajiv arrived there in the spring of 1998 accompanied by his wife and our mother, who were with him throughout the treatment he was to undergo, and they were there at the very end. I visited him, but as I was unaware that his condition was so critical, I returned to Delhi and kept in touch with what was happening from over there. The family did what they could – our mother would even cook him Indian food in an attempt to get him to eat.

Rajiv was a fighter and so even those closest to him never quite realised quite how ill he now was. The Cleveland Clinic, meanwhile, was doing what it could to treat him and the next thing they did was to fit him with an LVAD (left ventricular assist device). In essence a sort of artificial heart pump, the device is put into action when the heart has become too weak to pump blood around the body and is sometimes given to people who are waiting for a heart transplant, as Rajiv still was, to buy both the patient and the doctor a little time. Just as I was to do a short time later, Rajiv was waiting for a heart to become available, which meant that matters were now out of everyone's hands – the doctors, family, everyone. It was simply a question of waiting to see what would happen next and the LVAD was the best chance of keeping him alive at that point. But it was not to be. Complications occurred during the course of the operation, which was extended by about five hours as the doctors battled to save his life.

Hope exists until the moment that it can exist no more and so we were all desperately praying that Rajiv would pull through and that a replacement heart would become available before it was too late. Sumant remembers: 'We were all hopeful. He had that mechanical aid installed that assisted the heart as an external pump as he wouldn't have survived without that assistance. It was meant to operate as a bridge to a transplant because the transplant itself is a complicated process, depending on your luck and the availability of a donor who will be able to provide a match. Timing is everything. In essence, it is the sickest people who are eligible for a transplant but, at the almost-end stage, there are people who need it more than you, so you have a small window between becoming sick enough and then becoming too sick for it. We all hoped the pump would get him through the next three to six months, when a donor might become available.' Sumant pauses and looks into the distance. We are all too dreadfully aware of what happened next.

In all, it took a few days for the end to come. Dhruv remembers that at times his father was delirious and didn't recognise him, but there seemed initially to be some improvement and the doctors even managed to get him out of bed to walk. At first we all thought the operation had been successful, despite the complications that had extended his stay in the operating theatre; so when, four days later, I got a call out of the blue to say he'd died as a result of complications arising from the operation, it was a complete and utter shock. We had previously consulted an astrologer in Delhi who said that if my brother crossed the twentieth of the month he would live but, with a horrible irony, it was on the twentieth that he died. 'It was awful,' says Sumant, with some understatement. 'We were all completely devastated. None of us had expected this.'

It is hard to overstate the shock the entire family felt at what was to come. 'He was doing fine,' says Rajiv's daughter Simran now. She remembers getting very upset about the way her father behaved after coming around from the anaesthetic, when he would say some very odd things. 'I was in college by then and I'd gone to the hospital to see him: he was sleeping but he opened his eyes and told me, "Study hard." I thought, "OK, he's not so great," but I wasn't worried – I was even chirpy on the flight back. But when I got back – he'd passed away.'

I was beside myself with grief. My heart, already weakened physically, now shattered emotionally into a million tiny splinters, but I had to move into action and tell everyone else what had happened. 'The news of his passing was conveyed to me by you,' says Mr R. K. Dhawan, his voice trembling slightly with emotion. 'I remember what a choked state of mind you were in as you simply could not believe what had happened. It was a terrible shock to everyone.'

When you have had such a massive shock, the body often goes into automatic mode and so it was that we all started making the relevant arrangements and embarking on the grim tasks of what had to be done. There was a funeral to arrange, formalities to be fulfilled and all this while none of us could really take on board what had happened – we had lost Rajiv.

Anita – supporting me as always in my grief – flew out with me to Cleveland to join Rajiv's wife Rita, their son Dhruv, our son Bhanu, who came to us from his college in Boston, and my mother. I remember seeing my brother's body in a cardboard box in Cleveland, where we held his cremation before returning to Delhi with his ashes. I was in such a state of shock and distress that the whole period is very blurred in my memory. Then, once we were back in India, we scattered some of his ashes in the holy Ganges and some in an estate we bought in the hills before Rajiv died. After thirteen days, as is the tradition, we held a condolence meeting for over 1,000 friends, family and business partners, after which the reality of the situation finally began to set in.

I was initially absolutely shell-shocked but, as that stunned disbelief began to wear off, a deep depression settled on me. My brother and I were so close in every area of our lives and now I was never going to see him again. When he died, Rajiv had just entered his fifties, no age at all these days. My mother Amrit had now lost her eldest son. For a parent to lose a child really is the most terrible thing to experience because it should happen the other way around. She has a picture of Rajiv in her bedroom to this day, but she never talks about him. It is clearly too painful for her to speak about.

Everyone agrees that this had a terrible effect on my mother and set in process an inexorable decline that continues to this day. She is still alive and living in India, but she is nothing like the life force she once was. Grief can destroy a person and in this case it did. Dhruv, still reeling with the shock and the pain of his own loss, recalled, 'She never recovered from my father's passing. My grandmother was a real force within the family and it destroyed her. She used to talk all the time, was as sharp as it came, an amazing woman. She kept the extended family together. But despite all that strength and energy, she was completely destroyed.' And matters were to be made even worse when just eight months later my own health collapsed, almost certainly as a result of the grief and strain I felt at Rajiv's death, and I too would need a new heart.

When an unexpected death occurs, there is no end to the traumas and problems that arise and, in this case, there were any number of layers to contend with, from personal suffering to practical concerns. The ripple effect of a seismic shock like this continued to spread out over the water and various other things were now becoming clear. The first was that Rajiv's death had also profoundly stunned the employees in the company, whether or not they had actually known him. When a powerful figure disappears, it creates instability within the souls of everyone and I knew I had to try to reassure them as best I could. I had everyone gather in the corporate office and addressed them, assuring them that life would carry on, as it always must. It is not overstating it to say that Rajiv was in some ways a father figure to everyone. When you lose a figure with that much charisma and inspiration, people are left feeling vulnerable and helpless and it was now up to me to do what I could to start the recovery process for us all.

Suddenly, it was now only me at the top of the company. Until Rajiv's death, it had been the two of us, doing everything together. We had established a way of working together that meant both of us always knew exactly what we expected to be doing. Now, that was completely gone. Of course other senior company officials were a great help, but I now had to establish a new way of doing things. Dhruv was shortly to come and start working in the company full-time and I hope that that in some ways helped him through this awful time – but he was only just finishing college himself and couldn't possibly have been expected to step into his father's shoes. It is at times like this that you can feel very alone, but Anita was always there, supporting me and giving me the strength to go out and shoulder what had hitherto been a joint burden on my own.

In the immediate aftermath of my brother's death, as everything was still sinking in, I asked my sister-in-law Rita, Rajiv's widow, to come to my office to talk about him and that helped a little bit. I felt his presence once or twice in my dreams. But I miss him and I will always miss him. Another part of my heart had gone. Little did I know, though, when I had met Dr Mancini and her colleagues in the course of trying to find a heart for Rajiv that soon – very soon – I would be back in Columbia. The heart I had been born with had had enough and Rajiv's death was what finally broke it. Very soon, I would be in need of a new heart of my own.

CHAPTER 7

THE HEART OF THE MATTER

And so, to the heart of the story. It concerns many hearts and one man who has encountered more than most in his life is the man who has come to be known as The Wizard of Oz. He is the man responsible, literally, for giving me a new life: Mehmet Cengiz Oz, Professor of Surgery at Columbia University Medical Center. The author of numerous publications and the recipient of numerous awards, and the man who performed my heart transplant, Dr Mehmet Oz was born to Turkish immigrant parents, Suna and Mustafa Oz, in 1960, in Cleveland, Ohio, and was brought up in Wilmington, Delaware, although he often visited Turkey when he was growing up.

Hearts run in the family. Dr Oz Senior had been a heart

surgeon before him, at Wilmington Medical Center, and the young Oz decided he would follow in the paternal footsteps, studying at Harvard University, the Wharton School and the University of Pennsylvania School of Medicine. These days, Dr Oz Junior is well known to the American public as the popular presenter of television's *The Dr Oz Show*, which started in 2009, having come about after a series of well-received appearances on Oprah Winfrey's show; but back then, when I had my operation, he was known only as one of the most skilled practitioners of his trade.

Dr Mehmet Oz came into the story when I was so critically ill that my medical team were seriously concerned that I would not make it through the night, much less survive for many years afterwards. I had been admitted to Columbia and now time was becoming absolutely critical, the search for a heart was urgent and surgery could not be postponed much longer. Had no heart become available, I would have had to be fitted with a mechanical device because my own heart really was close to beating its last. However, this would have considerably lessened my chance of survival.

'I first met you around eight o'clock on a Friday night when I was called by Donna Mancini to see a gentleman who had had prior heart surgery who was dying of heart failure,' Dr Oz says matter-of-factly today, seated in the offices of *The Dr Oz Show*, at Radio City Music Hall on the Avenue of the Americas in New York. 'The details included the fact that both sides of the heart were failing, which meant you had a lot of fluid in your belly, which makes the operation harder. You were a bit malnourished; the pressure in your lungs was very, very high but the pressure in the rest of your body was very low, which is the worst combination possible.

'So on paper, anyway, you definitely would not consider doing anything like a hernia operation on Bunny, much less operate on his heart. The question was, was there anything we could do to keep you alive? Because we thought you would die that evening, maybe the next day but not too far in the distant future. You would not be able to sell life insurance for Bunny Choudhrie. I remember presenting the reality, the dire reality, of what we were facing as physicians and I was actually considering putting a mechanical pump in you. In the middle of all this, I learned that your brother had died at the Cleveland Clinic of a similar type of problem and that you had hoped your heart failure would get better by fixing one of the valves, but it hadn't worked as you'd hoped.'

In other words, we had reached a total crisis point, and if the operation had not been done immediately (and successfully) I would have died. It was as simple as that. Dr Oz told me later that, although he had been impressed that I could take an analytical view of the situation, he also realised that Anita had effectively taken control, made all the arrangements for my hospitalisation, and had done everything to ensure that I had the operation and was as comfortable as possible in these utterly dire circumstances. There was no question at all that I would die without the operation. If a heart became available, Dr Oz rated my chances of survival as high as 75 per cent. But at that stage no heart *was* available and with a mechanical device instead, my chances would have been about 50 per cent. 'I was left believing it would not have a favourable outcome,' Dr Oz says.

But then, at the very last minute, my new heart came into the picture. As I said at the beginning of this book, I have no details at all about the donor, but I do know some very basic facts: that the heart itself came from a twenty-year-old person who was killed in a motor-vehicle accident in the American Midwest. (If I had wanted to investigate further even those basic facts could probably have led to the identity of the heart donor, but I chose not to.) The location raised some issues in itself with Dr Oz taking a risk in accepting it. Dr Mancini explains: 'The heart he accepted came from the Midwest, so the travel time is longer. The window is four hours from the donor to the recipient.' But we were past the point where we could wait for a heart to become available closer to the hospital:

my old heart had given out and my body needed a new one right now. In fact, the timing of the heart becoming available was astonishing: usually, when a patient needs a new heart they have to wait six to eight weeks, which in my case would almost certainly have been fatal. But this heart came up in the early hours of the Sunday morning – just a day and a half after Dr Oz and I first met.

Another factor that played a part in making the operation possible was that, at the time, Columbia had been expanding its heart-donation programme, making it known far and wide that if a heart became available elsewhere in the country that could not be used locally, they would send a team to fetch it as soon as they were given the news. The centre was getting calls from as far away as Florida if a heart became available that didn't match the body size of a local patient, or was perhaps the wrong blood-group type, and was benefitting greatly because other hospitals that were geographically closer had not been so aggressive in their pursuit of viable hearts. 'We were always the back-up centre,' says Dr Oz, 'which made it a little more difficult as in some ways it created higher-risk situations. But it was still better than the situation that you were facing, which is that I would have had to put an LVAD into you.' That was the same operation that my brother had undergone and it had not been successful. And whatever the risk from accepting a heart that was further away and had thus been out of a body for longer, the fact that the Columbia details had been circulated far and wide was a strategy that was going to save my life.

My family's reaction when they discovered a heart had become available was, according to Dr Oz, 'happy, obviously, but almost Zen'. 'It was equipoise. Everyone recognised that this was the first step and it's a marathon, not a wind sprint, which means you have to save your energy – which also means saving your happiness, as it's part of your energy.' In fact, throughout my time in the hospital, both before and after the operation, Anita had managed to create an atmosphere of acceptance, meditation and calm. We had all reached the stage of believing that whatever happened next was in the hands of a higher power.

The valve operation had been done about eighteen months before the transplant, and the fact that it had been so recent created yet another problem when it came to the forthcoming surgery. For a good eight or nine years after a heart operation, there is a lot of scar tissue and, according to Dr Oz, after just eighteen months, 'it was like cement. And the heart's all swollen, on top of which, it ticks. So if you cut into the cement and nick the heart, it pops. You get blood all over the place, the patient dies and everyone goes home.' He allows himself a rueful grin.

On Sunday, 17 January 1999, Columbia received a

telephone call informing them that a heart had become available in the Midwest. Dr Oz picks up the story: 'The hospital scrambled the harvest team, as it is known, consisting of a surgeon and two assistants. They rush to OR [the operating room], pick up bags of ice. Cardioplegia, the material we preserve the heart in, is very important; every centre makes their own. They put it in a bucket with ice, all the equipment they needed, all the sutures they needed, the cannula, all the pieces of plastic – you want your own stuff. You don't want anyone else's stuff. You have about fifteen minutes and, by the time you're done, there's an ambulance downstairs waiting for you, which takes you to the airport, where you fly out.' A plane flew out from Columbia to the city where the heart was situated, a two-hour flight. As the team left the hospital, I was brought down to the operating room.

When the team arrived at the hospital housing the heart, they were required to make their own evaluation of the donor, to ensure suitability for the transplant, and so met the donor coordinator, who was in charge of getting the family to sign off on everything that is required (they never meet the actual family). Once established as being a viable option, the donor was taken straight to OR and, as the Columbia team entered too, they rang the home hospital and said, 'We're in the room now.' As this was happening, I was being immobilised back at Columbia. The donor team opened the chest and visualised the heart, meaning they were ready to go ahead; while back in Columbia I was put on a stretcher and taken to OR, cleaned and made ready to go but not put asleep yet. In the Midwest, meanwhile, the donor team harvested the organ.

'They clamped the aorta and at the same time sliced the vena cava in half,' says Dr Oz. 'That exsanguinates the patient [drains him of blood]. They put the heart in the cardioplegia and made sure it arrested normally. They had to move quickly because if they had been sloppy it would have killed all the other organs such as the liver and the kidneys and they were probably already going elsewhere. So you have to be thoughtful. The moment they stopped the heart and they knew it had gone well, they notified Columbia and we put you to sleep. The organ was now harvested and they immediately left the room; usually in cases like this all the other teams are now working around the clock to harvest their organs. Everything was coordinated: as they said "ETA five minutes", we opened your chest. We knew we only had two hours so I had to get your heart ready, but that meant digging it out of the cement block of scarring from a year and a half earlier. This had to be done very quickly but carefully, so as not to damage it. Then, and only when the plane landed here, we stopped your heart. We never do this until the plane lands because there have been times when the plane has crashed. They often have to leave in bad weather because there's often been a crash which has provided the heart that's been caused by that weather but it makes it more perilous for them too.'

The plane landed: now Dr Oz started to stop my heart prior to cutting it out. 'It takes about twelve minutes to get from the airfield to Columbia so we have twelve minutes to get the heart out of the chest,' Dr Oz recounts. 'The harvest team came into the room just as I was taking the last cut of the bottom of Bunny's heart. To cut the heart out, I clamped the aorta and I had two cannulas in the inferior and superior vena cavae [the two large veins that carry the blood through the upper and lower regions of the body]: I snared those so all the blood was being bypassed around the heart; then, leaving as much of the aorta as possible, I carefully cut away the heart.

'I cut the aorta, the pulmonary artery, the superior vena cava, the inferior vena cava and the pulmonary veins. Once it was all out, there was a big hole, a gaping space there because it was a huge heart, the size of a basketball that used to be in your chest. It was eerie and I still find it eerie; everyone would feel the same. At this stage in a transplant you are looking at a person who is alive but everything is gone from their body. They literally have no heart. There's something very poetic about the heart: it's like a python. It's coiled up in someone's chest. It's very intimidating when you first start working with it and then you realise it's as scared as you are. But this heart had failed you so it came out as the new heart was coming in to the operating theatre. It was in a red igloo cooler. The assistant got the heart out of the bucket and then we began to prepare the heart for its new body. It was a race.'

My new heart had now been outside a human body for over two hours and Dr Oz and his team were working fast. 'The most important thing is that the heart was cool in the igloo cooler, wrapped in multiple bags of ice and water,' says Dr Oz, very animated as he recalled the operation which had been going on for some hours. 'You know the heart is going to warm up as you put it in the patient, so I moved expeditiously, no wasted movements. I put in the first stitch at the very back, the furthest away, between your left atrium and the new left atrium in the donated heart. I took a very long suture [surgical stitches] – it must be long to reach the bottom of the chest and you put lots of sutures in. As I was going around, I was quickly sewing the back of the heart in. As I got to the top I tied it down so at least your new heart was now connected, which on the surface is good but in reality is dangerous because now warm blood is coming in and warming the heart up. So I very quickly sewed the inferior cava, the superior cava, the pulmonary artery and the aorta. As the aorta was being finished, the heart was really getting warm, so I tried to get as much air out as I could as air is devastating. The heart desperately wants to get blood back now and any air in the aorta will go down the coronary arteries and block the blood supply. And that will kill the heart.'

Dr Oz got the air out, took the clamp off and my blood rushed in to begin to resuscitate my new heart. 'There's a very tense moment when you think, is the heart going to beat, to fibrillate [quiver with an irregular rhythm], will it turn into a stone?' recalls Dr Oz. 'Primary graft failure is not uncommon because something in the blood might reject that heart. You can never one hundred per cent know that won't happen. Or sometimes you hadn't preserved the heart well or something was going on with the other patient you didn't know about that results in the heart being dead. So everyone said their prayers and waited. And then I took my finger and tapped your heart, hitting it with about twelve volts. Then I used my hand and started to massage it because you don't want it to fibrillate. I always massage the heart because it gives me control: I know if it's full, if it's turning hard, if it's getting rejected – I can feel it in my hands immediately. If it fibrillates I'll shock it to get it to stand still and then I'll train it with my hand to get it to beat with me.'

After about a minute, during which the operating theatre was rigid with tension, my new heart began to follow a rhythm. The relief among those present was palpable. 'In your case, your heart snapped back,' recalls Dr Oz. 'Within about half an hour after putting the heart in you started to come off the heart/lung machine and as surgeons we don't really know if the operation has been successful till we do that. Your heart began to fill up with blood and actually started working for the first time again. But this is another critical juncture. As you put the blood in, you have to monitor whether it begins to distend? Stop working? Does it fibrillate? Then you get an echocardiogram [an ultrasound scan of the heart], which reflects whether the heart is actually squeezing or just lying there? Yours squeezed beautifully. It was almost jumping out of the chest. It was contracting beautifully, the valves all worked, the muscles were fine. It was why your recovery was so seemingly effortless: you had a powerful heart and your body just loved it. You adopted your new heart.

'You become a chimera with your heart if you're lucky,' Dr Oz continues. 'Some people are continually fighting the heart, attacking it with their immune system. But you responded in the way your family did when they found you were getting a heart: meditatively, thoughtfully. In a similar way, your demeanour to your heart was like that. You accepted it as a precious gift, your body treasured it, wasn't going to abuse it. Your body was able to make peace with the organ. From the moment the blood surged into the heart when we took the clamp off, the heart was being exposed to your immune system. Your cells were starting to take up residency in the new heart.'

The operation itself took about six hours but in total the whole procedure, from when I was taken into OR to be prepared, to the time in the recovery room where my family was allowed to see me, lasted about twelve hours. I was not the first person to receive a heart transplant, of course, but I was another example of the almost miraculous work that heart surgeons can perform today. There was a complete taboo about doctors touching a heart until about fifty years ago because if they did so the patient died. And they had no ability to keep the patients breathing so doctors attempted to avoid this at all costs.

But this began to change when, in 1931, Dr John Heysham Gibbon, an American surgeon from Pennsylvania, who studied at Princeton University and Jefferson Medical College of Philadelphia, began with the help of his wife Mary to work on the development of a heart-lung machine: a patient of his had died during cardiac surgery and Dr Gibbon had been certain they would have survived had there been a machine that could have artificially maintained the circulation of the blood.

It was not until 1953 that he had managed to perform a successful operation with such a device: Cecelia Bavolek's heart was attached to a machine and she survived the forty-five-minute operation, thus revolutionising the field of heart surgery. Meanwhile further huge advances were being made by Dr Clarence Walton 'Walt' Lillehei, a surgeon from Minneapolis who attended the University of Minnesota: in 1952 he participated in the world's first successful open heart operation using hypothermia. In 1958 he was also responsible for the first use of the pacemaker.

'Lillehei, who I got to know, would do cross circulation, which means you would take the mom and take her blood and circulate the child with the mother's blood so you could stop the child's heart and fix it,' says Dr Oz. 'It was a hairy operation because you had a mortality rate of two hundred per cent potentially with the patient and his mom. And it happened sometimes, too. But these folk had the guts to go back and do it over and over again and the most difficult thing, Lillehei told me years later, was to go back and do it again when you'd lost the first patient.'

That tradition of pioneering surgery continues to this day, but while doctors have made astonishing leaps forward in so many things, there still remains something special in their relations with the heart. 'When you touch the heart you still feel that sense of sacredness,' says Dr Oz. 'You appreciate how unique it is to have the opportunity to do something that mankind has never done before: touch the heart and not kill the patient. It's pounding away in your hand. It is like a serpent: coiled back, full of muscles, intimidatingly strong.'

Do hearts have personalities? 'Most hearts are conical,' says Dr Oz. 'They tend to snap out of the chest, jump out like powerful athletes. People who have had coronary disease: their hearts are like weathered seamen, worn out a little bit. Hearts like your old heart are hearts of desperation. They've done all they can to keep pumping and they're on their last legs. It's like a marathon runner at the twenty-sixth mile. There's nothing left. And you can almost count the number of beats they have left in them. You probably had a couple of hundred beats left.'

The operation was done: I had survived. Still unconscious, I was wheeled into the recovery room, but we were still a long way from being out of the woods. The first six hours after the operation are the most dangerous: potential problems included excessive bleeding – 'all these little tributaries become streams and they tend to bleed more' – and in my case the failure of the right side of the heart. 'The pressure in your lungs was very high,' Dr Oz explains. 'The new heart wouldn't have had a strong right side, it wasn't used to pumping against pressures in the lungs so the new heart might have been uncomfortable and unhappy and might have got mad about it. Then there was the danger of possible liver failure, kidney failure, bleeding. But in your case we used medications to address the issue of potential right-side heart failure and you got through the process.'

Dr Oz remained very involved in my case over the next year as 'a lot of the problems that happen in the first year are related to the surgery.' I did indeed develop pneumonia, 'which is a good example of what can happen. A lot of times patients get pneumonia as they don't have the right amount of acid in their stomach. They give you a medication to prevent you getting ulcers and that lets bacteria grow in your belly. And then if you're being put to sleep the saliva goes back into your throat and it goes into your lungs. It's called aspiration pneumonia. You will usually bring an infectious disease specialist in who will suggest further medication.'

Asked about the fact that I was to make a full recovery (after some issues along the way) Dr Oz glows with the kind of pride that a teacher would have in a star pupil. 'I can't emphasise enough how much sicker you were than a patient usually going for a transplant,' he says. 'Even though you survived you didn't just waltz through it. You were dealing with a lot of baggage because your body was not in any way ready to survive. It was checking out. Remember that throughout human history anyone as sick as you would have been dead within twenty-four hours.'

So, to the big question, why did I survive? 'A lot has to do with connection,' says Dr Oz thoughtfully. 'With a great many patients who survive, they're not ready to go, they have unfinished work and most frequently that means the people in their lives, family, the kids. So they're not ready to say goodbye. If your heart has a reason to keep beating, it will. And yours did. I've had other patients who should have done fine after their operation but no one visits them and no one comes to say hello. They sort of melt away into the bed, dissolving away.'

That didn't happen to me. Surrounded by a loving family, cherished by all of them and above all nurtured and cared for by my wife, one thing is quite clear: Anita is the reason I survived.

CHAPTER 8

A NEW HEART AWAKES

As I lay in post-op, gradually beginning to come round, my family had spent a very tense day waiting for news. It had been a long operation and Anita, my mother Amrit, Bhanu, Anita's brother Anil, and other members of my family, spent a fraught time sitting in silence, waiting for news. 'I certainly wasn't chatting: I sat there, praying all day,' says Anita. 'Just praying and praying and praying. When Dr Oz came out in the evening, he was looking so pleased. I've never seen a smile break out on anyone's face in such a way. He said, "It's gone really well, the body has accepted the heart." His whole face was lit up with a big smile.'

There were smiles on both sides: 'Dr Oz said he'd never seen a smile break out on anyone's face as it did on mine

– my face literally lit up, he said,' Anita continues. 'He told me I could go in and see you in a couple of hours, so after you were moved into the recovery room, I went in. When I walked in you were conscious but very swollen. But the first thing you did when you saw me was to put your thumbs up and whisper, "Hi. I'm OK. I'm fine."'

Indeed I was alive. My new heart was waking up and meeting the woman who had done so very much for me, without whom I could not possibly have got to this place. Previously my heart had expanded physically because it was breaking down. Now it expanded spiritually because of the emotion I felt.

As I began to regain consciousness, I could vaguely hear the doctors in the background, debating the amount of immunosuppressants I should be given in order that my body would not reject the heart. Dr Mancini came to see me shortly after I had been wheeled out of the operating theatre: 'You did beautifully post-op,' she tells me now. 'Mehmet did an excellent job and the heart worked well. Initially you were a little bit slow, with bad dreams and delirium, but once this was resolved you did excellently.'

I cannot pay tribute highly enough to Dr Mancini. When the crunch finally came and my heart failed me, it was Dr Donna Mancini, who had fought so hard to save my brother's life and who now did the same for me. It was she who got me to Columbia, she who put me under the care of Dr Oz and now it was she who was to supervise my recovery, constantly monitoring my condition and calling in other experts when they were needed, which indeed they were.

'The first time I met you it was as the devoted brother of Rajiv,' she says now, thinking back to all those years ago. 'You contacted me again in 1998 when you were having very serious problems. Heart disease can be genetic, so I wasn't too surprised that like your brother you were having problems, although I was more surprised when I learned that the problems were different. I brought you to Columbia by which time you were extremely ill: you were on intravenous medication and suffering from severe heart failure. You had to go on the transplant list; you were not a good candidate for bridging with mechanical support due to the prior mitral valve surgery. A transplant represented your best chance of survival.' I didn't drink or smoke, which was a help when I went on the list. And as so many people were to comment, I was certainly fortunate in one respect. Dr Mancini noted that in the desperate weeks that followed, 'Anita was always at your side. She was very devoted.'

Dr Mancini herself came to Columbia in 1993: she and Dr Oz started working closely together right from the start. 'We shared patients, including those who needed mechanically assisted devices and patients with heart failure. We often consulted one another on how to proceed. Mehmet helped enormously in getting the transplant for you: it was a long distance procurement, but the constraints of time were offset by the fact that it was a young donor.'

After the operation Dr Oz was constantly present to make sure my recovery was happening apace, but it was now Dr Mancini who took over the day-to-day running of the show, which was a source of great comfort to Anita. 'Dr Mancini is not only very approachable, but she's amazing,' she says. 'She's a woman of few words and she'd be very cautious even about telling me the good news because until the patient was actually up and out of the hospital she remained cautious, but it was astonishing what was happening. They were doing biopsies of the heart every week to make sure it was going well and there wasn't any indication of rejection. The signs were all very positive.'

As soon as they were able to, the medical staff got me first sitting up in bed, then moved to the chair by the bed and then finally standing, another crucial step on the road back to recovery. The first time I attempted to stand up I collapsed and ended up on the floor as my muscle tone had gone, but it wasn't long before I felt a familiar determination to get back to normal as soon as I could. One of the earliest excursions from my bed was to make my way to the bathroom: at first I felt extremely weak but after just a few steps, I thought, 'Yes, let's go.' After that I felt Dr Mancini, in particular, was determined to push me as much as she could.

Anita remembers the first week after the operation well. 'There were fluid retention issues, the kidneys weren't functioning well and your heart had irregular beats,' she recalls. 'The doctors kept adjusting your medications to keep your body calm and the drugs were making you sleepy although you were only really heavily sedated for the first few days.' I was having serious problems with my kidneys, and there was a real chance that I would have to have dialysis, until another member of the team, Jery Whitworth, stepped in and was able to help me using slightly less conventional methods that somehow did the trick. I will speak more of how Jery helped me, not only with this particular problem but a further happening that came to terrify me, in due course.

As my recovery began to gather pace, I developed pneumonia from an organism called *Nocardia*, although there were initial concerns that this could have been something much worse, this time affecting my lungs. Dr Oz's comment that one of the many reasons that Dr Mancini is so good at her job is that she is all over every aspect of the patient's health and calls in further experts immediately to assist in diagnosis and treatment could not have been better illustrated now, and so I was introduced to the next one of the team at Columbia who were helping to bring me back to health.

Larry L. Schulman, M.D., is Professor of Clinical Medicine at Columbia University, College of Physicians and Surgeons, and Attending Physician, New York-Presbyterian Hospital in the City of New York. He is also Medical Director of Quality Assurance, New York-Presbyterian Hospital. His speciality lies in pulmonary disease medicine – lung disease – and I first encountered him several days after the transplant when Dr Mancini asked him to do a consultation on the back of a suspected respiratory infection as I had been coughing up thick yellow phlegm.

Initially there were fears that the prognosis would be very bleak indeed. As Anita said, I had been in to have regular myocardial biopsies in which a small piece of heart muscle is removed for examination: this involves lying flat on a table, numbing the neck and chest and then having a catheter threaded into the heart through a vein or artery, a process known as cardiac catheterization. In the immediate aftermath of the operation this was done every week for the first month before decreasing it to twice a month for month two, then once a month up to month six before reducing it to every two months to month twelve, then every six months to month twenty-four, then once a year, then once every three years and finally it stops all together – unless you have been through a stressful period of some description and it starts all over again. It is an unpleasant procedure and somewhat painful.

Back then, right after the operation, it was done on a weekly basis. Frequent chest X-rays were done. And in the course of these tests it emerged that I had spots on my lungs. The initial fear was that I had survived the heart transplant only to end up with lung cancer, and I was sent for another battery of tests. These included a ventilation scan, in which you breathe in radioactive gas through a mask while lying under the scanner. To everyone's great relief, though, it turned out that the problem was eminently treatable and much less serious than we had at first thought.

'My initial impression was that you had pneumonia,' Dr Schulman, a compact and dapper man sitting in his office in Columbia, recalled a decade and a half after the event. 'It turned out that you had *Nocardia*, an unusual pathogen that I had encountered a few times but not very frequently.' No-one could know for certain quite why I had developed this, although it does strike people with a weakened immune system. Dr Schulman continues, 'This is very rare in normal patients and relatively rare in immuno-compromised patients. For you it was both unusual and surprisingly soon after the operation. But we treated it with the specific antibiotics and about six weeks after the operation it was gone.' Many heart transplant patients will develop so-called 'opportunistic' ailments after the surgery as they are taking such high levels of drugs to suppress the immune system, but in this case the issue did arise surprisingly quickly.

Dr Schulman is rueful about the fact that, of all the organs that can be transplanted, his own speciality – lungs – are the least likely to be successful, while hearts are middling, after the most successful, kidneys and livers. He has continued to treat me for other ongoing ailments such as bronchitis and respiratory problems in sometimes darkly comic circumstances, such as when I was in Japan some years later and suffered some problems. A Japanese physician who was treating me rang Dr Schulman. The only problem was that the Japanese doctor didn't speak English and Dr Schulman didn't speak Japanese, so he had to get someone to tear around the hospital to find a Japanese speaker to translate. 'The doctor in Japan was overwhelmed,' he remarked.

As with so many of the doctors who treated me back then, Dr Schulman and I developed a friendship, seeing one another socially from time to time as well as for the regular check-ups that I was to have with him three or four times a year from then on. He remembers the moment that we really first clicked, crediting it with being the moment when he knew I would survive. 'The ward had a party for all the transplant recipients to celebrate St Valentine's Day because of course Valentine's Day is all to do with hearts,' he recalls. 'You came down in your robe and I remember being impressed with the way you held yourself and from that moment on I thought you would do well. It was partly because of your mental attitude but it was also to do with the strong degree of support you were receiving from your family, which helps a great deal.'

Neither Anita nor I ever got discouraged at this time, no matter how difficult it sometimes seemed to be, because we continued to put our trust in a higher being now. I was in the care of some of the best doctors in the world: from now on in it was fate. 'We were both in a situation where we were almost expecting complications, be they major or minor, but at the same time your brain was fine, your limbs were fine and now it was really just the doctors' job,' Anita recalls now. 'We were now enjoying the fruits of what we had been through and we had total confidence in the doctors, so we just let them get on with managing everything. We took it in our stride.'

As my recovery continued, Anita made a great effort to maintain an atmosphere of calm around me. Dr Oz had spoken of the feeling of zen with which my family and I greeted every development that came up and that was in no small part due to Anita, who made sure that the attitude was one of meditation and prayerfulness all round. 'She turned to a spiritual healer when the prognosis first came through and offered her prayers to God, something she continued to do once you were in hospital, reading to you after the operation from the *Bhagavad Gita*,' says my brother-in-law Anil. 'The consultants coming into the room would comment on how peaceful and calm it was compared to the other rooms they saw on a daily basis.' This calm was maintained when visitors came – although there was the odd ruction, of which more in the next chapter – and it created a feeling of acceptance as to what was happening. Dr Oz also mentioned that some people's bodies rejected their new heart, possibly almost subconsciously, but my body was only too happy to accept mine.

Dr Lee Goldman is the Harold and Margaret Hatch Professor and Executive Vice President for Health and Biomedical Sciences at Columbia University, where he also serves as Dean of the Faculties of Health Sciences and Medicine at Columbia University Medical Center. He was not in situ when I had my operation, taking up his post in 2006, but we have become good friends since then. 'It was an excellent outcome: a combination of good doctors, a good and careful patient and good luck,' he says, sitting in his comfortable office in the very heart of the Columbia University Medical Center. 'Good patients have to take good care of themselves and understand their bodies. They have to achieve an equipoise between looking after themselves and not actually driving themselves crazy. Clearly, people talk differently about heart transplants [from other organ transplants]. It entails a whole range of emotional and philosophical elements – it is a big deal.'

Dr Goldman emphasises strongly that although excellent medical care is essential to survival in a situation like this, it is also up to the patient to do everything they can to aid their own recovery. 'Some people can inappropriately feel they're immortal,' he says. 'Then they go crazy with worry. Some transplant patients come in here because of what they have done to themselves, whereas with others, it's just the luck of the draw, which is what happened to you. There's no point in wondering why something like this should happen to someone who has taken good care of themselves – life isn't fair and as doctors we just try to take care of everybody. One of the metaphors I sometimes use to tell people is that you have no control over the hand you're dealt, but you do have some control over how you play that hand. You've played your hand very carefully.'

Is there any conclusion that can be drawn about this particular story? Dr Goldman, who presides over a large department in an academic teaching hospital located in one of the poorer areas of Manhattan, smiles. He has seen every conceivable type of ailment, and any number of patients who ask why this has happened to them, and if he has any theories about any of this in the greater scheme of things, he's not prepared to say. 'The positive moral that we can draw from this story is that at the time of this conversation, you've had sixteen years of life that in any prior era and in most other places you would never have had,' he says now. 'You've seen your kids grow up and you have three grandchildren. There are things you can't do but you can do most things. You received a gift.' I did. The gift was pounding inside me as I thought about that, the gift that all these years later continued, with every beat that sent the blood around my body, to go on saving my life.

★★★

Time passed and after about a month I was allowed to leave hospital, shortly after that Valentine's Day party, but I was still told to stay in New York. The first three months after the operation carry the greatest risk of rejection and I was not going to be able to leave the city until that amount of time had passed. Anita and I settled into our hotel with its spectacular views out over Central Park, while Dr Mancini continued to monitor my every move. I was continuing to receive very large doses of steroids to suppress the immune system, alongside dacluzimab (Zenapax), an immunosuppessive drug which targeted activated cellular receptors responsible for the proliferation of cells that produce rejection, CellCept and a battery of other medicines. The biopsies continued, although with not quite the same frequency, and I was treated for hypertension.

Otherwise, though, life began to resume some degree of normality, although by now I was beginning to be plagued by terrible visions which I will describe in time. Our hotel was located at the other side of Central Park from the hospital but we were not too far away and we were very comfortable: we could take walks in the park, cook in our own kitchen and take advantage of all the facilities of the hotel.

According to Anita, it was not long at all before I began to feel a new lease of life. 'You had always had such a fiercely independent personality, but for a while you had had to become dependent on me for all your care,' she tells me now. 'But suddenly, you realised you were alive. You had seen your brother succumb to illness so you knew what could have happened, but quite suddenly your confidence became much more buoyant and you very quickly got back to work. You didn't want anyone to stop you and I didn't want to stop you. So I just made sure that you were eating properly, getting your medication and resting enough, but it was so good that you were becoming active again.'

The bond between Anita and me deepened more than ever during this time: the medication I was on would sometimes affect my mood but Anita was always there, stoic in her support, as our relationship became ever deeper, stronger and more understanding of one another. 'You never complained, you never felt sorry for yourself, you never voiced any frustration as such,' Anita says. 'If you were feeling anything there might have been the odd moment of irritability but you tended to make a joke about it, about all the medicines and supplements you had to take.'

Another person who came into our lives at that point and is still there is Kathleen Ullmann, a gentle and caring woman who is a massage therapist with a speciality in craniosacral therapy, which seeks to relieve pain and tension by manipulating the skull and AMMA, a form of acupressure, and reflexology. 'I was working in Columbia Presbyterian Hospital as one of the massage therapists in the then integrated medicine program,' she recalls many years later. 'At that time we would offer fifteen minutes of massage therapy and after that it was up to the patient if they wanted to see us again. It was a challenge when we first met because you'd just had your chest cracked open and your heart cut into and your body was trying to adjust to a newly transplanted heart so even a massage at that point could have been difficult for you. But I used a therapeutic gentle technique.' The first time I had a massage from Kathleen I was still wearing a heart monitor and we could both see my condition stabilising as she went on.

We actually first met a couple of days after the operation when I was still in a lot of pain and although I was conscious I was very groggy. 'You were depleted,' Kathleen says quietly. 'But when I asked you if you wanted the treatment you nodded. At this stage after an operation the body is still very much in fight or flight mode, but this type of therapy helps bring you back into a state of relaxation and enhances the healing process as it eases the diaphragm.' It helped so much that I started having daily massages; 'I started trying to make everything very peaceful,' Kathleen adds.

Both Dr Oz and Anita thought it would be a good idea for Kathleen to continue to visit me once I got back to the hotel, and she noticed a huge difference in the atmosphere. 'When we first met there was a greyishness surrounding you,' she says. 'Now although you were still very weak, there was a vibrancy in the atmosphere. I also felt a sense of reconciliation and harmony: your body was finding out who that new part was that had come to stay.'

Kathleen stopped working at Columbia in 2008 and is now a chaplain in the archdiocese of New York, but she comes to tend to me and all the other members of my family every time we are in New York. 'I've treated all the family and I have seen what a deep spiritual component there is to your wife,' Kathleen says, smiling. 'And I have only ever known the new Sudhir Choudhrie. I'm curious about who you were in that other time. I see a man with a sense of humour and largesse, someone extremely driven but also extremely disciplined. Massage is a very underestimated therapy, especially in the United States, which has a Puritan element to it, where the negative impressions about massage therapy and other forms of body work are gradually being dispelled. These therapies do help.'

As my new heart and I got used to each other, and my recovery progressed, I began to get restless. As soon as I was able I had started taking an active role in my work– in total I was only non-functioning for about two months. And I started to deal with the side issues that so many heart transplant patients must deal with: for example, the high doses of the medicine I was taking meant my skin became itchy: it dries very easily, to this day, and I have needed the services of a dermatologist as well. But other, unexpected consequences have been that my hair has grown thicker and faster than it had done for years, so much so that people have commented upon it. My nails started to grow much faster, too.

It should have been of no surprise, given that I had a healthy young heart now pumping the blood around my body with a vigour it hadn't experienced for some time. There were a lot of advantages to being 'an American at heart', which was a joke I made to some of my doctors, adding that I would have thought this might qualify me for a US passport. 'It might,' came the reply, 'but no one of foreign birth would ever be allowed a heart transplant in the States ever again.' I decided not to test that particular theory out.

And so my return to health continued apace, still not a sprint but a marathon, with much more to deal with in the years that lay ahead. But as my body recovered from the trauma of the operation, there were other people having to go through their own recovery, most specifically the members of my immediate family. The trauma had not been merely physical, but psychological, and it was going to take us all some time to digest what had happened – and carve out our paths in the years ahead.

CHAPTER 9

HEART ACHE

As the months passed and it turned out that my operation had been a great success, the burden of worry began to slip off all our shoulders. When we had passed the crucial three-month mark – the moment at which it became less likely that my body would reject my new heart – the future really did begin to open up again, with opportunities on the horizon and the globe opening up once more. Initially my whole world following the operation had been a room at the hospital and after I was allowed to go home, it began to expand to encompass the much wider horizon. Now it did so still more.

Anita, as always, played a crucial role in my recovery, leaving nothing to chance. Living in our home, she had everything cleaned and disinfected twice a day to combat the danger of infection. She engaged a separate cook for me and for a time my meals were cooked separately from those for the rest of the family. No one with any kind of cough or cold was allowed anywhere near me but at the same time she went to great lengths to make sure I didn't feel like an invalid. I was not able to go out and visit my favourite restaurants and so Anita tried to make our home cuisine as palatable as possible, encouraging the staff to cook new dishes and getting friends and family to come round as often as possible in a bid to make me feel more normal. Everything that could possibly be deemed to be harmful was removed from my presence and indeed under this strict and yet nurturing regime I began to recover, increasingly rediscovering joy in all the simple things in life.

The news of what had happened began to spread out beyond our immediate family. Mr R. K. Dhawan, always such a close friend of our family, was among those who expressed his shock at what had happened. 'I didn't know that you had almost exactly the same problem as Rajiv and that you would have to undergo a heart transplant,' he recalls now. 'After you told me I only prayed that everything would go well this time. I was in touch when you were in the hospital and Anita used to give me the latest information: I was so relieved and delighted to know the surgery was successful. I remember that I saw you when you returned to India after about six months: you were looking very cheerful although you didn't want to talk much about what you'd gone through.

I was alive, receptive to challenges and I wanted to get back to normal. But, inevitably, it could not be that simple for some things had changed irrevocably. It was not just my own heart that had been so burdened but those of the people around me too. Whenever any serious health problems present themselves to anyone, the ripple effect spreads out and other people suffer. 'No man is an island', as the poet John Donne put it, and those close to me had also, in various differing ways, experienced a great deal of pain.

Of all those who had been affected to one extent or another, one person never really recovered and that was my mother Amrit, although she rallied at the time of the operation, coming to New York with all of us and enduring the fear and uncertainty that were inevitable until the operation was over and could be considered to be a success. She didn't collapse as such at that point, but the strain and anguish affected the gradual deterioration of her health which lasts to this day. It had just been too much for her. From losing her husband so young – and she never remarried – to coping with my illnesses throughout my lifetime and finally to confronting the death of her elder son, life had already dealt her a series of very heavy blows. My heart failure, although I was to make a full recovery, was to be the final straw.

Something in my mother began to close down at that stage and she never really regained the lively personality she had once had. 'She was so close to certain family members and then she lost them,' Anita concurs. 'She personally nursed everyone but now I think there is a certain part of her heart that has frozen. But during the operation itself, she was very calm.' Indeed, she was to play a big part in comforting my younger son during the long months of my recovery after the operation, of which more later.

But as the years passed, my mother began to decline, a process which gathered pace as she got older, and will never now be the same again. She remains a force within the family, much loved and sometimes able to understand what is going on around her, but this sense that she has somehow given up on life is shared by other members of the family. 'The person most affected by all this, hands down, was my grandmother,' Rajiv's son Dhruv agrees. 'First by my father's passing and then by my uncle's illness. It is sad seeing someone with so much energy like this because it has destroyed her. Over the last ten years she has completely shut down.'

Those who are close to her have always sensed that events have been too much for her. Rajiv is always in her heart but she never speaks of him. And as the years have gone by, she has started to develop dementia so it is by no means clear that she understands now exactly what has happened. It is also possible that the stress of it all partially brought on this horrible disease, which robs the sufferer not only of memory but, as it progresses, their very identity. At any rate my poor mother remains the much-loved matriarch of our family but she is too frail now to comprehend these most tragic losses in her life.

Another person who has suffered greatly through all these travails is Anita. Always with me throughout all of them, making it her business to research my condition and in some cases protect me from its full extent, Anita has never wavered and never complained. But the sheer force of the worry she felt, and often still feels, has put her through hell. Her brother, Anil, who was with us in New York during the operation and stayed for about a month until it was clear that I was making a good recovery, remembers the effect it had on his sister when it became clear I would need a transplant. 'She was devastated,' he recalls now. 'She was very apprehensive, stressed and uptight.'

But Anita was also extremely practical and sought to alleviate her fears through activity. 'I would make notes in meetings with the doctors and keep a little diary so I would know exactly what to ask them next time,' she says. She began reading up on everything to do with my condition, as well as researching such topics as healthy eating to try to keep me in as good a condition as possible.

Anita is personally extremely health-conscious and keeps a very close eye on my diet and lifestyle to this day.

But it was very difficult for her: we had been married for decades now and to contemplate the potential loss of a spouse is traumatic at the best of times, let alone when you have two sons to worry about and other family members still devastated at the loss of Rajiv. Dr Schulman is one of several members of my medical team who witnessed at first hand the hardship this has visited on my family. 'I think it still takes a toll on Anita to this day,' he says. 'She doesn't like to let you out of her sight. She always wants you to exercise more, to walk more.' Some things, however, have not altered in the years since the operation took place. 'As a personality, I would not say you have changed," Dr Schulman continues. 'First and foremost you are a very strong family man and a businessman. Your dedication to your wife and children is quite clearly ingrained in your psyche.'

Of course, my sons were aware of the strain on their mother and they both had their individual take on it, although talking to them separately it is interesting that they came to one joint conclusion. 'I think it made her stronger, because she had to be,' says Dhairya. 'She's one of those people who loves to self-educate and so she educated herself a lot on the nature of nutrition, health, well-being and your condition. Bhanu and I were young so we used to tease her about it but today we understand it makes total sense. People these days are far more aware of the importance of a healthy lifestyle and she'd been talking about it fifteen years before.'

Bhanu agrees, but adds that the stress his mother had been under was so bad that at times he had been concerned it risked making her ill. 'She was very stressed, very emotional – anything would set her off and I think it affected her health. But she's not the sort of person who would express that to anyone. I often wondered if it would have been different for her if she'd had daughters as well as sons, because although we're very close, a daughter might have helped – because as it is she's always the one doing everything for everyone else.'

Dhairya also feels that the presence of a daughter could have supported Anita and helped her to carry the emotional burden, as well as giving her physical help with all the arrangements that had to be made. Of course there were other women in the family giving her all their support. But of the four of us in the nuclear family, three were men. 'Neither me nor my brother had a wife at the time, so she didn't have that female support around her,' Dhairya says. But perhaps the overwhelmingly male presence had its positives, too. 'I think the male support from me and my brother made her more adamant in her way of thinking, firmer and stronger, because she had to deal with three men,' Dhairya adds.

Dr Mancini, who has had a ringside view about how all of this has affected all of us, is succinct in the care Anita takes of me: 'Anita watches you like a hawk,' she says.

Both my children have also had many issues to contend with, albeit in different ways. To a child the parent is immortal and to discover the opposite can be a terrible shock. It is also very difficult for anyone to see their parent in a weak and vulnerable state and this is something both boys had to endure. Anita remembers how Bhanu reacted when they heard I would have to have an operation: 'Our elder son experienced a lot of strain,' she says. 'He was very disturbed by it all and felt that with you in such bad health, he would have to be the man of the house and potentially take over the running of the business. He wanted to leave his education and studies and start working.'

At such a tense time it was easy for everyone to get very upset and this is what happened now. 'One day when we were visiting you in the hospital, this turned into a full blown row,' Anita says. 'I just said, "No. You will finish your education, nothing's going to happen in the next six months. If you finish your education you will be more successful in life." He was extremely angry and upset with me and we had a big argument but I knew it would have been the wrong thing to do.'

I didn't play any part in this; I lay in bed and let them get on with it. In the end Anita prevailed. 'Bhanu was very much affected by all this', she says. He was there throughout the surgeries, on the fateful night when they found the heart and in the months afterwards he was flying into New York every weekend, which meant he missed out on a lot of attendance at university, but he made up for it somehow,' she says. 'This boy grew up in a hurry, with some intensity and it might have been the reason he joined the business as early as he did.'

When reminded of this now, Bhanu, who has played a pivotal role in the company since graduating and is now its Executive Director, smiles somewhat ruefully. 'At the time emotions were running wild and everybody thinks they're right in what they should be doing,' he says. 'I think my mother gave very sound advice. Thinking back it was the right decision not to leave university, not least because, what real value could I have added at that stage?' But it was an honourable offer on his part and Bhanu was having a very difficult time, juggling his studies and doing his duty as a good son. 'It did affect my grades and my ability to concentrate,' he concedes. 'Initially it was so stressful, because you would have good days and bad days and I was constantly calling and being told, "He's the same" – you don't necessarily know what "the same" means. It was tough emotionally and you did want to be there.' Fortunately Bhanu had a close circle of friends to fall back on in the immediate aftermath of the operation and he also received emotional support from his girlfriend Simrin, who was later to become his wife, although she was not at that time living close by. 'She was in London, which at least was closer than India,' Bhanu says. 'She gave me a lot of support.'

And Bhanu was also naturally worrying about his younger brother and the effect all of this was having on him. 'It brought us closer on an emotional level,' he says. 'Just the thought of the two of us possibly losing our father...' he trails off. 'I looked at my uncle and his two children and I thought, "How would our lives change?" Dhairya still had to do all the things that I was doing, like going to college and it made me very concerned about him. Generally, this whole situation made me a much more serious person, made me grow up faster than my peers and friends and had that not happened, who is to say what might have been?'

Simrin, to whom Bhanu has been married since 2003 and with whom he has a son – Kabir, five at the time of writing – remembers the toll it took all those years ago. 'I think in terms of Bhanu it's definitely shaped the person he is today,' she says now. The couple had known each other since they were children and so she is as best placed as anyone to see the difference in Bhanu turning from a 'lively, jolly, jovial character' to the more serious young man he became when crisis hit our family.

'He took on a huge responsibility at a very young age

and it was coming from this place of uncertainty,' Simrin explains. 'He took on a lot more than someone else his age would normally. They were unusual circumstances for sure. I think for Bhanu it affected him in a huge way, because for many years his only focus was his work. He became highly introverted on one level, for a few years he cut off all social ties, kept to himself, became very quiet and it is only in the last few years that he has started to come out of that. Dhairya was a little bit younger, still in school, so he was still in India. Because he was younger, the information that would reach him was relatively censored, so I think he was a little bit more protected. It's interesting to see the difference between the brothers: Dhairya was by himself so I think that he turned to his friends, he built some really good, strong friendships at the time, and that kind of forms his core as he is today. With Bhanu, he kind of went the other way – his only focus was work.'

Simrin also makes the point that there might also have been a cultural dimension to it all. We are a very close family and would have pulled together no matter what our background, but we come from India, where the traditions of a family staying together and looking after the differing generations is perhaps a little different from what it is in the West. It is not necessarily his Indian lineage per se that made Bhanu take on as much responsibility as he could as soon as he could – and indeed he is an ambitious man who would always have wanted to be involved with the family business. But the fact is that he felt it was his duty and that was perhaps influenced by his background.

'Throughout his twenties, he did not have the life of a twenty-year-old,' Simrin says. 'Naturally, that has to take a toll somewhere. It is an essential part of Indian culture that there are certain ties and associations to your parents throughout our lifetimes. It's kind of different from the UK from what I've seen with friends where you come into your twenties and move out; in India it's different, you could be married and with kids and your parents still living with you. You always have them close. For example, Bhanu moved to the UK and soon after you both moved to the UK, for the medical aspect of things, so he could be closer to America if there was a problem, and for the better healthcare. For you both, it was vital that you were very close to your sons.'

That is certainly true, although that would also have been true even if I had not had a heart transplant. We are a close family and would never have wanted to be far apart and Dr Mancini, who was very aware of what was happening to every family member, as well as me, her patient, pays tribute to Bhanu's strength of character at this horribly difficult time. 'Bhanu was always there, supporting his mum,' she says. 'His personality is more like yours, Bunny – he is very driven. But he was strong, calm and concerned, as was everyone involved back then.'

Dhairya was in a very different position. He was still at school in India and we thought it best to keep him there, although we got him to join us during school holidays as often as we could, but that entailed concerns of its own, with the two of us concerned that he might feel isolated and alone. There were many family members there to support him but his parents were far away, as was his brother, and his father, of course, was seriously ill. This was all happening during the middle of his adolescence, which can be a difficult time in itself, with exams coming up and any number of issues to deal with – but somehow Dhairya coped.

'This child spent a lot of time living alone through it all although of course he had his aunts, his cousin and his grandmother to give him support,' says Anita. 'I know he was frightened about what might happen, but he formed some very strong bonds with friends at the time who gave him a lot of support. His teachers were also very kind to him but it was a very difficult time for him and continued to be so for some years.'

Four years younger than Bhanu, Dhairya had friends, but not the emotional strength that a girlfriend or partner can impart. For a start, he was too young for a romantic attachment and secondly, he did not meet his wife Karina until some years after the operation. My operation really was having an impact on everyone, whether they were in India or with me in New York.

Dhairya came to visit us regularly and has since expressed the shock he felt on seeing me after the operation; even though it had been a success and I was on the mend, nothing can ever really prepare a child for proof that their parent is fragile and as susceptible as anyone to the tolls ill-health can take on life. Yes, I had had problems before, but nothing on the scale of this one. Teenagers have little concept of death – it is said that most people only lose their own sense of immortality after the age of thirty-five – and so even though Dhairya knew about my past health problems and knew I had had major surgery, the actual physical impact of a child seeing a sick parent will always result in trauma. 'When I first saw you after the operation, I remember you had a lot of water retention, but you had lost a lot of weight on the face,' he recalls. 'I was really happy to see you but at the same time it was such a shock to see you in that condition. It really shook me up.' Dr Mancini, that wise woman, commented, 'It must have been very frightening for him, alone in Delhi with the rest of you in New York,' she says. 'He was so young.'

Conscious that Dhairya was by himself and with all of us wanting to help him, once it had been established that I was on the mend, my mother Amrit would sometimes go back to Delhi with him after one of his visits, and that established a particular bond with him that lasts to this day. 'To be honest, while we were both there in Delhi, in the

144

house together, she had to deal with a sixteen-year-old boy which she had not had to do previously and while I'm not saying I was a bad kid, it couldn't have been very easy for her,' Dhairya says.

'She did an amazing job. I respected her and I listened, but at the same time she wasn't an authority figure as such – she didn't stand over me and make sure I did my homework. She just made sure that I was fed well and not getting into any trouble.' Amrit and Dhairya would talk about me and the operation, discussing any updates, but while she would get emotional at times, she held herself firmly in check, concerned about this young boy who was suffering because the rest of his family were so far away. 'She'd been through so much,' says Dhairya. 'I guess she was trying to be strong for me.'

Dhairya is characterised by some people who know him as more happy-go-lucky than Bhanu, although he too has turned into an immensely ambitious and hard-working man, but back then, he too felt he had to grow up faster than he would otherwise have done. It was that issue of confronting mortality again. 'Some years after the operation, I remember having a conversation with you about work and I said, "Look, what do you think about the next twenty years?"' he recalls. 'And you said, "I'm not going to be around for twenty years." I asked, "Why not?" and you said, "Because the average in heart transplant patients is ten." I didn't know how to respond, but you said it with such conviction and such acceptance it made it a little easier for me. You've always had such a zest for life, but perhaps in the wake of the operation it has focused you and made you think that we all only have one life and we should spend it doing what we love.'

Of course there was the wider family circle to consider as well. For my nephew Dhruv, also far away in India, it was a horrible reminder of what had happened to his own father less than a year previously and he was now experiencing yet another huge family trauma. He actually graduated a few months after his father Rajiv died and straight away came to work for the company – and I hope that being immersed in the family business helped him to cope with his own grief. But just eight months after losing Rajiv he was seeing a near-identical scenario: that I was in desperate need of a new heart. 'It seemed so unfair,' he recalls now. 'It was the same scenario all over again. It was back to New York and back to speaking to the cardiologists and searching for a heart. It was amazing to hear that they'd found one but on the day they performed the surgery, it was the darkest, scariest time. I was terrified.'

Dhruv was not just worrying about me: he was also shouldering the concerns of carrying on the business and although of course there were people who had worked in the company for years doing their part, as a close family member he felt particularly responsible. There was no-one else to do it: Bhanu was in college, Dhairya was at school and so was far too young anyway, and other family members were in New York with me, but as well as giving him the weight of responsibility, like Dhairya, he was isolated at this immensely difficult time. 'I would speak on the phone with Bhanu every day to get an update to see how you were getting on, but for a long time there was more anxiety than relief,' he tells me now. 'It was tough. I was far away, getting everything second hand and I didn't really know what was going on. I didn't know how it was going to go, either.'

Dhruv's sister Simran remembers a similar sense of shock when the situation became clear, although she actually felt a degree of positivity right from the start. 'When it began it was just awful, with such a sense of déjà vu,' she says. 'But this time round I had confidence in my own mind that it would be all right, because I thought, God cannot do this to us again. After my own father died I stopped believing in God for a time, but I thought this time it would turn out fine. I didn't believe in God for the longest time but then I began to think it's down to destiny. Whatever happens, happens for a reason and time does eventually begin to heal. You have to carry on. And now when my own daughter Sarena, who was born in 2012, asks me, "Where is your father?" I say, "He lives with God."'

Like most of us, Simran believes the whole episode drew us closer together as a family. 'So much had happened that we needed to be there for each other,' she says. 'When I first saw you after the operation, we all had to wear masks and although I wanted to hug you I couldn't – none of us could touch you. But there was such a sense of relief that it was going to be OK. I also could see your progress, too. Because I didn't see you every day, but rather every week or every two weeks, I was more aware of the changes than I would have been otherwise and by the time visitors were allowed everything really was getting better. I always felt that you had a level of acceptance about the situation which helped you to recover: it must be strange to come to terms with the fact that someone else's heart is in your body, but you accepted it and were positive about it. I also think the fact that we are an Indian family and provided each other with such a strong sense of support that it really helped.'

I really was on the mend now and increasingly keen on going back home myself as soon as possible. There was just one problem: I was increasingly plagued by inexplicable – and terrifying – dreams.

CHAPTER 10

BAD DREAMS

As time went by I continued to make a recovery and I could feel the strength returning to my body. We had settled in to our life in New York. Anita continued to provide the devoted love and attention that did so much to bring me back to good health, but then a setback occurred that was as terrifying as it was unexpected – so much so that according to Dr Mancini it actually temporarily delayed my recovery. It took the form of a dream, or perhaps a vision and it first happened about a month after the operation.

I was fast asleep when I quite suddenly saw the figure of a woman. She had black hair, and was sitting on the ground. I couldn't see her face as her hands were pressed up against it. The background was green, outside somewhere – I didn't know where she was but I knew it wasn't in New

York or India. And she was speaking. 'You promised me you would come back,' she said. 'I knew you would come back. You promised me you would come back.'

I didn't know who she was or what she meant but it was absolutely and utterly petrifying. I woke abruptly in a cold sweat, without a clue who or what this person was, although right from the start I wondered if it was someone connected to the person who had originally had my heart. A wife, perhaps, a mother or a girlfriend? I had no way of knowing. But from that moment on, I was plagued by these terrifying dreams, which haunted my sleep and waking hours over and over; so much so that I began to dread going to sleep for fear of what would come to me in my subconscious. Over and over she appeared, always repeating the same thing: 'You promised me you would come back,' she said. 'I knew you would come back.' By this time, in the anguished distress this apparition was causing me, there was nothing I wanted more than for her to go away. Very little frightens or unnerves me but the sensation this was provoking was sheer terror and I had no idea what to do.

Who or what was it? It is impossible to say. As transplant surgery has got more advanced and we have come to know more about it, we have become increasingly familiar with a phenomenon known as 'cellular memory', the theory that a transplant patient's personality can in some way be influenced by characteristics of the donor, with the transplanted organ in some way carrying a memory of the deceased person forward and transplanting new tastes and habits into the patient. There are all sorts of odd stories about people waking up after surgery able to speak a foreign language or possessing some particular kind of skill they never had before. In other cases they seem to have experienced a change in their personality.

This is not something that has been widely accepted by the medical community and in my own case neither I nor anyone else has noticed much of a change in me before and after the operation save for on the most trivial level, such as seeming to swap a taste for tea pre-transplant for coffee after it. Nor do most of my doctors give this theory about cellular recovery any credence whatsoever. Dr Mancini, for example, while deeply sympathetic, believes that the trauma sustained by the body during the operation, combined with the highly potent cocktail of drugs I was taking, might have had as much to do with it as anything else.

Dr Oz, however, has a slightly different take on this from many of his colleagues. While he dismisses the notion per se that this was another person's memory, he points out that in recent developments in the study of epigenetics, there is a theory that external or environmental factors can switch genes on and off and affect how cells can read genes rather than by changes made in the DNA sequence. In one famous example, they changed in the offspring of women who survived a terrible event in World War II called the Dutch Hunger Winter, which lasted from November 1944 to late spring 1945 and which involved near-starvation among parts of the population of Holland.

They also changed in these women's grandchildren. Although women who became pregnant during the famine had smaller than average children, as was to be expected, it later emerged that when those children grew up and produced offspring of their own, these children were also smaller than average – a more unexpected development. But we still know very little about this area and I simply don't know if it can explain what happened to me or whether something else was to blame. 'I think that the cells of the heart remember where they came from but I don't think it's quite the way many people envision cellular memory. It's much more subtle than that,' Dr Oz says. However, he concedes there could have been other causes: 'That said, high doses of steroids, the trauma the body goes through during the operation and the fact that sleep patterns are badly disrupted – something, after all, that we do to people when we torture them – could all have contributed to what was going on. The truth is that I don't know what that vision was,' he continues. 'Memories or dreams like this are impossible to explain.'

Dr Mancini strongly believed that in my current fragile state nothing should be done for a year after the operation because my body would not be able to cope. The visions did not happen all the time, but they continued for over twelve months, so she agreed that some kind of regression therapy could take place. The dreams were so vivid and so disturbing that I felt something had to be done about it and this was possibly not a case where conventional medicine could help. It was at this point that Gerard Whitworth, always known as Jery, stepped in. I already knew Jery: he was a part of my medical team and had been present during the surgery in a different capacity from the one in which he was about to treat me.

Jery was (and is) both what you might call a practitioner of conventional medicine *and* an ardent espouser of complementary methods; and at the time both he and Dr Oz were extremely enthusiastic about the idea that patients could and should have access to both. After the death of his own father, in 1985, Jery – who had initially trained as a nurse and had been running two jewellery stores – retrained as a clinical perfusionist, a member of the clinical team who specialises in ensuring that the oxygen reaches the patient's body through the blood, during the time when the heart is not actually functioning. He was there, as I said, throughout my surgery, our initial meeting being when, as he put it, he 'was wearing a white lab coat, with scrubs underneath and clogs on' – in other words, he was very much part of the conventional medical staff.

But Jery Whitworth was interested in other forms of medicine as well, most specifically complementary treatments. In 1994, he, Doctor Oz and Dr Eric Rose, the latter then Head of the Department of Surgery, founded the Cardiac Complementary Care Center within Columbia University's Department of Surgery. Jery, as one of the directors, spent the next few years building it up and exploring non-mainstream treatments, such as medical hypnosis, therapeutic guided imagery, acupuncture and other manual therapies like massage, acupressure and reflexology, plus movement therapies such as tai chi, qi gong and yoga. In 1999 it became a department in its own right at Columbia, and Jery, with a foot in both traditional and non-traditional medicine, was clearly an ideal person to turn to at this time of very great distress.

A gentle and empathetic man, Jery was not only aware of the physical aspects of what I would undergo during the operation, but also of how Anita and I were feeling before the operation was due to take place. Although we both knew it had to be done, I was naturally very anxious and Anita was terrified; but Jery's soothing presence helped both of us even then. Dr Oz, who was very aware of the turmoil that goes on in a patient's mind before an operation, suggested that Jery come to see us – although even he could not have predicted the longer-term help that Jery would provide.

'Dr Oz asked me to go and see you before the surgery took place. Anita was petrified and I could see both you and Anita had very depleted energy levels,' Jery recalls now. 'There was a very, very strong sense of your connection to one another – far more so than between most husbands and wives – but equally that meant that the two of you were experiencing the fear and anxiety before the operation equally strongly. I could sense you were two individuals who were looking for assistance in a cold environment, which entailed removing the heart from your body and putting a new one in, something neither of you had any control over.'

Initially, Jery was convinced something more than the nuts and bolts of conventional medicine were needed to get the patient to make a full recovery, and that was why he and Dr Oz were the instigators behind what had by now become the Columbia-Presbyterian's Department of Complementary Care Services. It no longer exists in exactly the form it did then, but it had been set up, Jery says, 'because I was worried about the sometimes cold and callous environment that medicine could seem to be'.

Jery had been interested in yoga and meditation ever since the 1970s and had impressed upon many of his colleagues the very beneficial outcomes these treatments could have. These were certainly not alternative treatments to be used *instead* of the conventional ones. Rather, they were augmentative therapies, to run alongside the conventional treatment the medical staff were giving, and used to alleviate pain and stress.

The first slightly augmentative treatment, for lack of a better phrase, that Jery practised came about after the operation itself, when Dr Mancini was supervising my care and when my kidneys were not functioning properly. As a result, I had so much fluid in my body that my legs had swollen up like tree trunks. This is a normal by-product of a heart-transplant operation but, equally, it is essential to get rid of the fluid and have the kidneys function properly again or I would have ended up on dialysis, which for a short time seemed a near certainty. Huge amounts of diuretics were being used to try to stabilise me but it wasn't working, one of the results being that I found it impossible to urinate, a situation that was both acutely uncomfortable and potentially dangerous.

This was the first time Jery's alternative treatment was used on me. He is able to harness the body's energy and the best way to describe this is that, as a demonstration of what can be done, he will sometimes hold his palm about an inch away from another person's palm and, although they are not touching, the sense of energy – something like static electricity – is palpable. He was going to use this ability to galvanise the body's energy on me.

Anita was present at the time and remembers it well. 'Jery said to Dr Mancini, "Can you just give me a couple of hours with him and, if you still need to do dialysis with him, he's all yours." He made me sit in the room on a chair,' she recalls, 'and quietly, with just the three of us, he took you into hypnosis. I myself started to fall into a deep sleep, but I was still aware of what was going on in the background. He took you on a journey and, after he got us to wake up, you started to release the bottled-up fluid.' Essentially, he worked on the energy level within my body with the effect that at long last I delighted both myself and everyone else by regaining the ability to urinate. Looking back on it, it seems an odd cause for celebration but after a heart transplant, the body malfunctions in so very many different ways that each sign of progress is a triumph. That was a physical ailment (one of many), but the spiritual one was about to emerge and Jery's help there was greater still.

Back in our hotel, I was walking again, slowly coming back to myself, but one absolutely crucial element of recovery is taking proper rest. And it seemed quite cruel that, increasingly, every time I tried to do so, that strange, unnamed girl returned to my dreams, jerking me out of unconsciousness, waking me up in a panic, covered in cold sweat. Over and over again, I shut my eyes and there was the girl with her face covered by her hands again. 'You promised you would come back,' she would whisper, over and over again. I woke up terrified, not knowing who or what this vision was and what it could mean. No one could explain it and no one had any idea what to do.

Anita, like me, could not get away from the feeling that it had something to do with the person my heart had come from. 'I definitely felt it was a past connection with the donor,' she says to me. 'They say it can happen and science can't prove any of this one way or the other and nor can the people on the medical side of it say there can be any connection, but alternative medicine does say something like this can happen. It is not like you to be frightened but in this case, when there's a foreign personality completely out of context, it can be very disturbing because it's nothing like anything you have within your family or friends. You weren't watching too many films or becoming haunted by a character you'd read about in a book – instead, you were being visited by something in a dream. It didn't help that you were physically weak at the time and so you were not strong enough to dismiss it, as you would have done under normal circumstances. You needed help.'

One year later, the person who provided that help was Jery Whitworth. Until now, with the possible exception of when he was helping to get my kidneys to start functioning again, he was working very much within the traditional medical framework – but now, we started on something radically different. And a decade and a half after the very much needed succour he provided, Jery says, 'I was stepping over a line. I released myself from the open limitations of how far I should go with a heart-failure patient. I went to a deeper level with you and I moved from being a person in a lab coat to a facilitator, someone who is attempting to build a relationship with one's internal healer.'

At the time, while my other doctors had been very sympathetic, no one had actually been able to do anything. I had told them about the dreams and they in return responded that these things did sometimes happen. But I was desperate and so the idea began to surface that Jery would see if his alternative methods could be of any help. I already knew and trusted him, which is essential where this kind of therapy is concerned and matters were by now so bad I thought they couldn't get any worse.

What Jery did was to take me through a form of regression. I went into a deep hypnotic state and I was asked where I was. 'In a park,' I replied, and I realised that by now I was a child. 'There's not that much – an older boy, an older man and an older woman. The man was in a black coat and the woman a white coat. I kept falling over.' And then I had another vision. A group of us were in a room and everyone was crying. Then I emerged from the hypnotic state and later when I was in Delhi told my mother about these visions and she told me that the first occasion I remembered was the day before my father died in a car accident when we were all playing in a park. The second vision was the day we received the awful news he had died. 'Who told you this?' she asked.

I explained to her how it had come about.

'That is exactly what happened,' my mother, astounded, replied.

I woke up, with no idea how long I had been under, dreadfully thirsty and after that I slept like a baby. I was exhausted, but there were no dreams because even if the regression had given rise to another sad memory, one of which I had been completely unaware until then, it had worked. The dreams stopped immediately and I have never been troubled by them since. And while I can remember what they entailed, the memory contains no fear. It was all rather extraordinary and according to Jery, it's the subconscious mind that is being explored during these sessions, which is why, when examining one very traumatic experience, details of another formative happening from my young life came out. But whatever the thinking behind it – it worked.

Jery himself remains publicly non-committal about this nightmarish vision. 'I choose not to express what I think it was,' he says. 'I don't know if we will ever get to the bottom of this kind of phenomena in my lifetime. In this case, you had a heart post-transplant, you were on extremely strong medication, and there were all sorts of chemical releases going on in your body. Perhaps it could even have been a latent memory. But what I do in these occasions is to allow someone to observe themselves in a detached way so that they can see whatever the feared thing is from a different angle. I take people to a comfortable place of awareness and the fear itself knows it is being listened to, sensed and heard. Then the fear begins to morph into something else and changes in a positive way. The fear dissolves and although the memory of what frightened you remains, the fear itself does not. You're not gripped by it any more.'

As for the fact that I was taken back to a seminal and profound early childhood moment, but something I had previously had no recollection of, Jery believes that this too is not surprising. 'People tend to regress to an initial sensitising event,' he says. 'Normally, what emerges is something that happened before they were eleven and the most common age range is between birth and the age of six or seven. During that time the brain is like an open hard drive: there is no filter. Everything gets burned into the brain but really painful memories get shoved down and a critical filter begins to form. It is common for someone to go back to a time that had a huge impact on their life and that they were unaware of until then. What I do is to facilitate people to do so in a safe way so that they are not reliving the trauma.'

I didn't see Jery for many years after he had given me such a huge amount of help. Our reunion, in the summer of 2015, was an emotional one. Both Anita and I feel that Jery is a remarkable man, while for his part, he could see that I had made a complete recovery, thanks in large part to him as he had helped to put the emotional suffering to an end. 'I was marvelling over how well he looks,' Jery told a friend afterwards. 'He was standing tall and erect with a full head of hair. Many heart-failure patients don't take responsibility as to how they will live their life fully afterwards, but Bunny should be the poster boy for individuals who have the possibility of having their life cut short. And, of course, a lot of credit must go to the support team around him; above all, Anita. He's doing it and he's looking great.'

It was to be a very long time before life returned to normal and at that stage, in the immediate months following the operation, it was not even clear exactly where we were going to live. India was still our home at that point but, for all its bustling glory, it is not the most sanitised place on the planet and Delhi is one of the most polluted cities in the world. Slowly, I began to think that London might become our permanent home: Bhanu had already set up residence there, it was a much cleaner city, with its own high standards of medical care should a crisis arrive out of the blue and it was halfway between India and the United

States, to which I would now return with a great deal of frequency as the doctors monitored my condition and ensured my recovery would continue to gather pace.

I already knew London very well: I had been visiting three or four times a year for decades and felt at home there. So another big change was to take place in our lives following the transplant: the United Kingdom would become our permanent place of residence.

Back then, in the immediate aftermath of the operation, I was becoming increasingly eager to get back into the swing of things again. I wanted life as usual to be resumed. That was not immediately going to be possible, though, as I was going to have to stay on in New York for nearly three months after the operation so that the doctors could monitor my progress during this crucial period.

What I needed in the meantime was a project to occupy my mind. Sometimes, when you are in need, life provides, and this is exactly what happened now. A friend was in town with an idea he believed might take off, but he had been doing the rounds of the banks and finance houses, only to encounter a wall of indifference. And then he asked if he could have a word with me. Anita was initially reluctant, but he repeatedly called, and so she relented and decided I was ready to face the outside world.

I listened with some considerable interest, because not only did I need something to work on — and in later years both doctors and my family said it almost certainly aided my recovery – but the prospective project sounded interesting and full of potential. It involved something that had been around for a few years by then, but only now were people beginning to realise the full extent of its potential. I'd heard of it too, although I certainly couldn't claim to be an expert. But that 'thing' the idea involved was certainly being increasingly talked about. It was called 'the Internet'.

CHAPTER 11

COME FLY
WITH ME

There's a problem with making a full recovery to health: it's dull. Until my heart transplant, I had always travelled a great deal, which became an important part of my life. But now, albeit for the best possible reasons, I was stuck in New York for a good four months. My doctors wouldn't hear of me travelling during that time and nor would it have been sensible: those early months after the transplant were crucial and, if anything had gone wrong, I needed to be where I could receive immediate help. But it could be a little tedious and the better I started to feel the more restless I became. You can only take so many walks in Central Park. As I said, I needed something to work on.

I am no computer expert – to this day I see technology

as something that happens to other people – but I can sense a business opportunity when it comes along and that is what happened now. The timing could not have been better, both in terms of a project coming along to engage my interest and in taking advantage of a new area that was soon going to dominate all of our lives. It came about as follows: a friend and entrepreneur called Dinesh was living in the same block of flats as Sumant and I knew him very well. Dinesh was educated in the UK and after leaving university went to work at IBM. But he soon decided that he wanted to build up his own business and, in 1980, with his wife Tani, started Dabin Travel Limited, a business selling travel tickets from a kiosk near Earl's Court Underground station in west London. Within three years, it was doing so well that it developed into Flightbookers, a fully-blown travel agency operating from three different premises.

It was around 1994 that the Internet started making its presence felt to a more mainstream audience and, while many people didn't see its full potential immediately, a few did. Dinesh Dhamija was one of those and, by 1996, he could see the potential success of an online interactive travel agency – an idea that is commonplace now but was revolutionary at the time. He came across an innovative IT software package that allowed customers to book transactions online, something which we might all be very familiar with today, but which at the time was unheard of. This was launched in the UK and Flightbookers.com became the first interactive travel website in the UK, quickly doing so well that it was obvious that it should be extended out across Europe. But this was easier said than done.

Dinesh started looking for funds for expansion. But he faced two problems: the first is that a lot of the funding providers he approached simply couldn't understand what a visionary product he was talking about because at the time the standard mode of booking journeys entailed a physical trip to a travel agent – or at the very least a phone call to one – actual printed tickets and the services of a travel adviser. And then the second problem: making it work.

The Internet has now become such an accepted part of our lives that it is often forgotten quite how fast it has grown from niche to dominant mainstream and quite what a bumpy period it had in making that transition. The Internet was a new and unknown territory just two decades ago and there were all sorts of early problems that doomed companies that were really ahead of their time.

But as we all know now, a revolution in the way we run our lives, including booking travel, was well under way. I, meanwhile, needed something to distract me. 'You were getting bored,' Bhanu reminds me. 'You weren't used to sitting still even for one day.' And I had been sitting still for months.

The timing for what happened next was right for all of us: in January 1999, around the time that I was being wheeled into the operating theatre for the procedure that would either save my life or end it, Dinesh was setting the wheels in motion for a very different chain of events. He set up a new venture called eBookers.com – although it was to be a while before that name entered common usage.

During March, as my new heart had started to get used to its new home – and vice versa – and I became increasingly keen to find an outlet for my growing energies, Dinesh came to the United States. He had done the rounds of private equity firms in the United Kingdom, without success, and so now came to New York to test the lay of the land: he needed someone who could be a strategic adviser to him. He needed someone who could think outside the box.

We had an initial meeting at my New York hotel, where Dinesh and I talked about what he wanted to do. 'I have no idea what this "Internet" is for; how does it work?' I asked him. 'I don't have a computer myself and I am absolutely computer illiterate'. Dinesh explained that this was an area with huge potential: where people could just log on to a computer in their own home, click on a site and buy what they saw, which in this case was flight tickets. It sounds self-evident now, but at the time it was pioneering and no one else, including a major airline he had also approached, would agree to finance the project.

Bhanu was there and remembers it well. 'Dinesh finished explaining and you said, "I don't know if I'm being stupid here, but if I buy my ticket online, how will I check in without a ticket?"' he recalls with a grin. 'In those days, you had to check in with tickets: they kept one half and you kept the other and so we went through the process over and over again. So eBookers was a tricky one but you believed in Dinesh and you believed in the future of the Internet. The Internet was starting to become the biggest phenomenon of the twentieth century and you somehow felt that it was going to serve people well. You also felt that people can make or break a business and you had confidence in the people here.'

As I said, this initial meeting took place two months after my operation and it needed some careful thought. I went off to discuss it with a few other people, including my nephew, Ashwin – who at the time was working with JPMorgan – who would go on to advise on the flotation later in the year. Ashwin joined Bhanu and me for a short meeting. 'This seems to be a great idea,' they said in unison. 'Let's go,' I said to Dinesh, telling him we would take this further when I returned to London, whenever that might be.

It wasn't to take very long. At last, I was to be allowed to escape my gilded prison and leave New York. Not only was I back up and taking an active part in the business but my life was in other ways getting back to normal once more. The good news was broken to me by Dr Mancini herself, and it related to Anita's birthday in April. 'You can give Anita a special birthday present,' she said. 'You can go back to London.' And so, just under three months after the operation that had saved my life, that is exactly what we did.

It was wonderful to be in the city where I would shortly make my home, and wonderful to taste my old life again, working, travelling and looking ahead. Once in London, I had more talks about the opportunities afforded by eBookers. Everyone was cautiously optimistic so I went ahead and came on board as a non-executive director. I still had no idea what the Internet was but by now it was very clear to me that we were on to something special . . . which was proved to be true.

It was also exactly what I needed to give me a boost. 'I could see the glimmer in your eye, the interest you had in understanding this business you had no idea about, the technology you had heard about for the first time,' Bhanu recalls. 'You were still in a recovery period, but being able to talk about a business opportunity instead of blood pressure, doctors, and medicine was a huge change and so good for you. It probably played a part in aiding your recovery and was so useful in that it came along at just the right time.' My doctors were largely in agreement: they too realised that although rest and caution were necessary, at the same time, I needed a way back into my way of life. Everyone needs something to get up for in the morning, something to get the juices flowing and in my case it was and always has been work.

Dhairya, of course, was still at school and far too young to be personally involved in the business himself, but he was very aware of this exciting project that was taking shape in New York and was in no doubt that it helped my recovery. And his very youth perhaps gave him a greater insight into what was going on than would have been the case otherwise, because it was the coming generation who were the ones to start using the Internet before anyone else – indeed, they grew up with it.

'You've always been interested in new things, new industries, and I think that gave you an insight into the technology world,' Dhairya tells me now. 'As a business it had huge revenues. Because it was so early it was one of those businesses where the world had not migrated and moved into where it is with technology today. But it was still a service where people were consuming a product, consuming a service: consuming travel. That was still the core fundamental of the business. I think that excited you, that it was a tangible product. We had a number of hospitality investments at the time and you understood it had a lot of relevance to the hospitality industries.'

For me, it was almost like a true learning experience, a hands-on learning experience. It was new for them too because of the Internet Age. I wasn't working at that point but it was very much me asking them questions about how the company worked, because we were selling tickets online – but I didn't know how that system worked. At the time they were very much pioneers in their work.' They were, indeed, and this was about to be brought home to the wider public when the company floated, as it was to do in November 1999.

Anita witnessed all this at first-hand and with it saw me returning to the person I had been prior to my illness. I had depended on her in a way that I had never done before and the bond between us continued to deepen and grow closer. Some marriages come under intense strain after a heart operation but, while no relationship is ever completely perfect, the opposite was happening with us. But as our relationship became stronger than ever, so I felt the need to return to our previous way of living together as a couple and my new involvement as a non-executive board member was a way of bringing that about, too.

Anita was as happy as I was that everything was coming back to normal. 'You have always been a fiercely independent personality; I wouldn't say independent in that you wanted to live a life apart from other people, just an independent personality, which is different,' she tells me now. 'You were very dependent on me for all your care – medical, physical comforts, but you suddenly realised that you were alive and you'd seen your brother succumb to the sickness. And now your confidence was buoyant because you'd realised you'd got through it. So, you went back to work and you didn't want anybody to stop you and I was really happy about that. As long as your food was right and your medicines were on time and you were eating them and you were resting – it was good for you to be so active.'

Indeed, life was to be lived again to the full. Businesses were to be built, opportunities sought out and a pioneering Internet travel business was about to become one of the major success stories of the early dotcom era. 'The enthusiasm and interest you brought back into your business and your new businesses were amazing,' says Anita. 'This was within the month you were still in your hospital bed, when you made the decisions. I've always been a silent supporter – I don't phrase it vocally all the time and that was the kind of support I gave you. Neither was I a pessimist, so there was really no change in your outlook on life – in fact there was more enthusiasm than before.'

In the autumn of 1999, eBookers was separated from

Flightbookers and in November floated on the Nasdaq in New York and the Neuer Markt in Germany. Within four years it was the largest Internet portal in Europe, growing from pretty much nothing to over $1 billion in revenue.

Ultimately, in 2005, it was sold to the travel giant Cendant and it is now part of the giant Orbitz Worldwide. It certainly marked a significant turning point in my own journey back towards health.

★★★

For now I really was making a good recovery, but although I was able to resume work fairly quickly, I discovered that I had to make some other changes in my lifestyle. If you have been given a second chance then you have to do everything to live your new life with your new heart in as healthy a way as possible – and so I now found myself making changes to my diet and daily routine, which I would recommend to anyone in a similar position. Even the smallest changes can make a big difference: if you cannot walk a quarter of a mile in less than five minutes, then your chances of dying within the next three years is 30 per cent higher than if you can, so even if you do no other exercise, it pays to get out there and walk.

It is not always easy to stick to them, but I found that I had to integrate five major lifestyle changes into my routine and they have helped me to stay in good health.

The first of these is that all important thirty-minute walk every day. This will have an immediate effect on the health of your heart, your weight and even your sex life and in the longer term a daily constitutional may help to fight the threat of Alzheimer's disease. The reason is that it decreases the level of Apo E4 in the blood, which is the protein that causes a build-up of amyloid-beta in the brain, the cause of Alzheimer's. So walking leads not just to a healthy heart but a clear brain.

Another important step is to floss your teeth as well as brushing for two minutes, for brushing removes only 60 per cent of the germs from the teeth, which can lead to gingivitis, tooth loss and heart disease. I also drink at least two cups of green tea a day, something that is common in India and should be established elsewhere, for green tea is younger than brown tea, which means it doesn't have the same oxidising (i.e., ageing) effects. It also maintains high levels of polyphenols, which give you a burst of energy with only a third of the caffeine.

It is important to get enough sleep – seven to eight hours a night – because our bodies need to repair cells, process information and boost growth hormone levels, which decrease as we age and we need them for vitality. Too little sleep is also linked to heart disease and so, for obvious reasons, I make sure that I am well rested. And finally another Indian practice – meditation for five minutes a day.

Yoga, prayer and meditation are all widely practised across India and are a real help in reducing stress and finding your true path in life.

Managing stress is important, especially when you have a new heart you want to take care of. A certain amount of stress can be beneficial, in that it raises our adrenaline, focuses our thinking and can galvanise us to make bold, life-saving decisions, such as swerving out of the way of a car. But, equally, chronic stress can lower immunity, opening us up to the threat of cancer, heart attacks and even accidents. I have developed two ways of dealing with this: the first is deep breathing. It helps to lie on the floor with one hand on your stomach and the other on your chest: take a deep breath in while pushing your belly out to a count of five and then slowly exhale to a count of seven while pulling the belly button in. I try to do this several times a day. Secondly, meditation also helps: try to clear the mind of all distractions, by repeating a word such as 'ohm' over and over, and try to do this every day.

In the wake of my heart operation I was strongly motivated to return to my work as soon as possible. I have been fortunate in that I have always known what I wanted in life. But to make a full recovery it is essential to find a purpose in your existence concerning what you want to do, places you want to see and any untapped passion you might want to follow and the following exercise helps. Take a piece of paper and draw a box with an amoeba inside it. The box is your job and the amoeba is you. How much of the amoeba lies outside the box? Do you have interests outside of work and, if so, what are they? If you are not spending as much time as you would like on your outside interests, what is holding you back? Finding this purpose helps you take control of your life, a crucial step towards recovery, and your nearest and dearest can help you access that too. Ask people who are close to you to describe you in one positive adjective. Do they say you are wise? Kind? Try to be this every day.

Anita has made sure that I follow a healthy diet since my operation and I have often been asked what I eat that makes me look so well. The first step to healthy eating is to be mindful, which means not eating in front of the television or while taking phone calls. Sit down with someone and chew twenty times before swallowing, which will slow you down so the hormones that drive hunger will have time to catch up. It will also force you to focus on the taste of the food and realise its sacred nature.

I don't focus on my weight but I do eat a morning meal that is rich in fibre or protein to slow the progress of the food through the small intestine so you feel full for longer and don't start filling up on caffeine or junk food. There are five healing foods you should try to eat every day and in the following quantities: seven portions of whole grains, four of fruit, five of vegetables, two of low fat dairy and one of tree nuts. A serving is the size of your fist or a deck of playing cards. On top of that you can eat anything you like as long as your waist stays less than half your height. Do, however, try to avoid simple carbohydrates – food just made of sugar – which can be difficult after a heart operation as steroids often make you crave these foods. Planning ahead can be a great help.

★★★

Another sign of my recovery was the renewed interest I was taking in the world and one manifestation of this came some years later, around 2003, when I became involved with the Liberal Democrat Party in Britain. By this time Anita and I had already relocated to the UK. I had increasingly wanted to become more involved in politics and the scene in the early years of the twenty-first century in our new home was an interesting one.

In 1997 the Conservatives (under John Major) had suffered a massive defeat at the hands of Labour, something that was going to take them eighteen years to reverse and by the time I became active New Labour, and in particular Tony Blair, were at the absolute height of their powers. But the Labour Party was not of interest to me: the Liberal Democrats seemed far more interesting for any number of reasons and we met some of the leading lights of the party, including soon-to be leader Nick Clegg and Lord Clement-Jones, and the relationship developed from there.

One of the reasons I decided to become involved in the Lib Dems was that they were a small party and I could see that my input of ideas would be part of building their policies going forwards. I had always been interested in politics: when I was at college I joined the Student Union and was elected to the college council, which always had to contain one student; my grandfather had been the chairman of the college management committee at the time and was frequently subject to complaints about me from the principal of the college, so I was used to the hectic nature of political life.

After my heart transplant I wanted to do something more for both charities, of which more anon, and politics. The Liberal Democrats asked me to become involved in building relationships within the Asian community. There were still some internal matters I thought it best to allow the party to sort out for itself. I stayed away from the leadership race in 2007 in which Nick Clegg took over from Sir Menzies Campbell, but I played a role in helping to collect funds, bringing people in, making introductions and helping the party move from a campaigning pressure group to the mainstream.

I wanted to help the Lib Dems prepare to play a part in government, which they did after the election in 2010.

A large group of us had dinner just before the election, with many of the major players on the scene at the time in attendance, and we were able to discuss how they might serve in government with the Conservatives, not least because I was privy to a lot of meetings going on at the time. I was able to talk from my experience of seeing the bigger picture, which is something that party leaders need but do not always get. I also always told them when they made decisions I didn't like, such as the U-turn over students' fees. Senior figures in the party have been kind enough to mention that I always gave them support and stepped in when it was needed.

I was delighted when, in November 2015, the new leader Tim Farron asked me to be his Adviser on India, a role that I was only too delighted to accept. We both put out statements to mark the event. Tim said: 'India is a key strategic partner for the United Kingdom and the British-Indian community contribute so much to our country. I am determined that the Liberal Democrats do all we can to maximise the economic, cultural and social benefit of these relationships. Sudhir has been a committed supporter of the Liberal Democrats for many years and I look forward to being able to draw on his vast business experience, unparalleled network in both the UK and India, and wise political counsel.'

I replied: 'I have long believed that the Liberal Democrats best embody the internationalist and pro-enterprise values that characterise the British–Indian community and I am honoured by Tim Farron's decision to ask me to fulfil this role. India, with its ever–vibrant and expanding consumer market of over 1.2 billion people is slated to emerge as the world's third largest economy by 2030, which makes the country extremely attractive for investment. It is critical that both India and the UK collaborate on a common agenda of growth.' The Lib Dems remain a crucial part of the British political scene and I look forward to playing my role in the years that lie ahead.

CHAPTER 12

LIFE, ACTUALLY

Although the operation was a great success and my life in the decade and a half since has been as full and rewarding as it ever was, there have been huge changes that I have had to come to terms with: changes in lifestyle, medical conditions that have been exacerbated by some of the treatments I have been forced to have, and the need to adopt a totally new way of life. When you are well and healthy you think nothing of strolling down the street, popping into a shop or attending a sporting fixture, but all these activities and very much else have become fraught with complications for me.

I have to plan in advance now in order to avoid situations that could entail serious medical problems and many activities are now simply out of bounds. But while there has been a price to pay, how could I ever complain? I have been given so many more years in which to see my children reach maturity, get married and have children of their own, with all the thrill that being a grandfather entails, many more years to spend with Anita, my wife and the woman responsible for giving me a reason to fight back to health once more. Any small personal sacrifices have more than been made up for in the years that would not have been mine if I had lived even a couple of decades before.

But these adjustments have not always been easy and nor could I have foreseen quite how much they would come to dominate my life. For a start, I will be on medication for the rest of my life, to guard against infection, to stop my body from rejecting my new heart even at this late stage, and to deal with all manner of complaints and issues that arise from having had one heart ripped out of me and another installed in its place.

And although there have been some very positive physical side effects courtesy of my energetic young heart, there are some irritating problems as well, such as the fact that my body sometimes produces small growths which have to be surgically removed. They present no threat to my health but are a small annoyance. This happens about once every two years and they can be got rid of under local anaesthetic, in a procedure that takes about 10 to 15 minutes, after which I am in the clear – for now. After a while, it happens all over again.

And, although I travel, in some ways life is not as spontaneous as it once was. In every area of life I have to exercise constant caution: when I have dental treatments, I have to be given 3000mg of antibiotics to avoid the risk of infection, and in addition to this I have to take twelve pills in the morning these days – two in the afternoon and another five in the evening. I go to New York every three months for a check-up with my team of doctors at Columbia and once a year they run the full battery of tests and checks to make sure everything is working as it should be. To avoid the risk of the body rejecting the heart, my immune system has been suppressed through various types of medication, resulting in the constant risk of problems with thyroid and blood pressure.

Other problems include the fact that my skin is very sensitive these days: it can dry up in patches, which discolour slightly and can be itchy, and I have to see a dermatologist to resolve the problem. And the health of other people is now also a matter of concern in another complication that I would never have thought about previously. The problem is germs: infection has to be avoided at all costs. I cannot be around people with even a common cold: it risks an infection that, in my case, could be extremely serious and so family, friends and colleagues are all aware that if they feel a case of the sniffles coming on, then they should stay away from me. What may seem trivial to them could be catastrophic for me.

That in fact was one of the major factors in deciding to move from Delhi to London, which Anita and I did in the early years of the current century. Indeed, although I was allowed to leave New York four months after my operation, it was several more before I returned to the country of my birth. And so London seemed the perfect place to live: Bhanu had made it his home and Dhairya was shortly to do so and it is halfway between the United States and India. In the meantime, I also get medical attention in London. I have a cardiologist in the UK and my GP monitors me under advice from the doctors in the United States. But the constant risk of infection means that if I fly on a commercial airliner, I have to wear a face mask. So much has changed and yet, in terms of re-establishing my old lifestyle, so much has remained the same. I have learned that when you receive a new heart you walk into a whole new world, as well.

My habits have changed. Before my operation I went through a great phase of drinking five or six Diet Cokes in a day: that has stopped completely and I now have hot water with ginger in it or hot mint tea. At parties, I confine myself to water. I have reduced my sugar intake all round and cut out gluten. I have to be careful what I eat – seafood, of course, is out of the question and Anita keeps a close eye on my diet. Nothing can be left to chance. When I'm invited to dinner parties, I have to be cautious without wishing to upset my hosts, so I tend to eat beforehand and just play with my food – apart from anything else, I can't risk accidentally eating seafood as my allergy is so bad that even if my knife touches fish my throat closes and I stop breathing. I have to carry pills and a spray with me to counteract that if anything happens, and sometimes it does – Anita's brother nearly had a heart attack when this happened to me in a restaurant and had to get me back to my then-flat.

Of course there have been sacrifices: I miss going to the cinema, going to football matches and shopping malls. But these are minor matters compared to what has been given to me. That heart transplant didn't just save my life: it gave me a whole new way of living, opening doors that so recently seemed to be firmly and irrevocably shut.

But I am as familiar with the inside of an operating theatre as I ever have been and that is partly as a result of all the medications I have to take, which have gone on to produce further complications in themselves. Although the risk of my body rejecting the heart falls with every year that passes, that risk remains and not only do I have to swallow vast numbers of pills every day but the types of medicines I have to take can be widely different, including heavy doses of steroids and anti-allergy pills when I am being put through a barrage of medical tests which protect me from the side effects when I have to take iodine. They do have some side effects: the steroids make me very alert and the anti-allergy pills make me sleepy, so it can all be a bit of a merry-go-round. The steroids have another very common side effect, however, and this can potentially be much more dangerous: osteoporosis, the weakening of the bones, which causes them to lose density. This is commonly known as 'brittle bones' and it means they are more liable to fracture. This is exactly what happened in 2007 when my left hip collapsed and I was forced to undergo an operation to fit a replacement.

It was yet another trauma that I had not been expecting which landed me, severely debilitated, back in hospital for a time, although on that occasion the recovery period was mercifully a lot faster and the operation, while a serious one, was not on the same scale as the heart transplant. I had been feeling a pain in my hip for about two years when I was on the Glacier Express from Zermatt to St Moritz to look at the spectacular view it afforded of the mountains. The crisis, when it came, took the form of a strong and very painful jerk in my hip; I ended up back at Columbia where I had the hip surgery. The operation, which usually takes four hours, in actual fact was over in forty-eight minutes and I was up and about once more within a month and a half.

Of course it was nothing like as serious as my

recuperation after the transplant but once again I had to force myself to go from bed-bound to active as quickly as I could. My recovery was swift and this was partly due to my doctor, Dr Macaulay. The day after the operation he had me on a walker and a week later, when I was out of hospital and back in my hotel, Dr Oz came for lunch, took the walker away, gave me a stick and said, 'Now walk.' Then he took the stick away and got me to walk straight. I went through a lot of reflexology, physiotherapy and massage, with sessions at least once a week, and these treatments continue to this day.

And the litany of operations has gone on, although I take it in my stride and the outcomes are mainly very beneficial. In 2010 I had cataract surgery, with the result that in my mid-sixties, not only do I have a young and efficient heart, but I see better than I have done in years. Two years later, my body reacted to all the cortisone injected into me over the last few years, slowly weakening my bones and joints. On a fateful, cold night with acute pain and discomfort in my groin, I lost consciousness and collapsed against the entrance door of our friend's home during a party. I hit it so hard I broke the metal door stopper and had all forty guests in a total panic. Anita was in shock. She turned to our friends, who are doctors, for assistance. She thought it was my heart. The ambulance arrived within a few minutes. They were fantastic, their response and that of the paramedics was superb. They rushed me to Chelsea Westminster Hospital.

The emergency team kept me overnight for monitoring, and were hugely comforting to Anita and me. Our doctor friend stayed in the hospital with Anita until my medical condition was stable. We requested the emergency team to speak on the phone to the transplant team and Dr Mancini in New York to keep checking on the medications they could administer to me. A few days later we left for New York at the request of Dr Mancini, to come for further examinations.

The medical analysis showed I had multiple hernias, which looked treacherous because there were so many. The femoral artery running down the groin – the largest artery found in the femoral region of the body – was trapped in the herniated muscle. Thus, the lack of blood to my heart and brain was the cause of my blackout and pain. This very intricate keyhole surgery, which lasted four hours, repaired five tears in my abdominal wall.

It took months for my body to heal from this long procedure. Now, I have to and always will have to be very cautious on climbing steps and carrying anything more than two kilograms in my hands. This episode, and the subsequent weakening of my body structure and performance, was a traumatic experience for both Anita and myself, although one to which we swiftly adapted.

The important thing, as always, is that I have energy and take as active an interest in work, charity and politics as I ever did. Life continues to hold challenges, with so much to look forward to in the years ahead.

★★★

But the years have brought shocks, some terrible ones, with them as well. Advances in medicine have moved on hugely in the decades since the leaky valve in my heart was discovered when I was still a young boy: back then the know-how to perform a heart transplant did not exist anywhere and, when the time came for my own operation to take place, the expertise was not there in India. Now heart transplants are done all over the world with increasing levels of success as all our lives are changed by what doctors can do. And it is possible the heart issue has been in my family a very long time: my paternal grandmother died in her mid-fifties after a heart attack, although, since this happened in the 1950s, no one was aware of what might have caused it. My father's youngest brother also had a heart condition, although in the event he died of pancreatic cancer, but these days, of course, the medical science is there to deal with all of that.

The fact that my heart problems might have come down to a congenital defect has become of increasing importance to my family in recent years. It seems I have a mutation in the titin gene, which has been linked to heart failure and it appears that Rajiv might have had the same thing too. As a matter of routine, therefore, my children and Rajiv's children have all been tested.

Three of our four children were pronounced to be completely in the clear but, in 2014, a discovery shocked and upset us all: it emerged that Dhairya also has the mutation. This does not mean that he will develop heart disease, but it does mean that he might. He has responded with calmness and a level of maturity that could not be more worthy of praise and is, indeed, awe-inspiring. The intense shock I felt on hearing this resulted in some sleepless nights. However, I knew I couldn't help him by remaining in such a state so I started trying to think about it in terms of solving a problem. After all, when my own first diagnosis came through, it meant that we were forewarned and thus forearmed; we all feel that this is also true of Dhairya. Far better that he should know about his condition early on and so start to make any lifestyle changes deemed appropriate, as well as starting a thorough monitoring phase with the same team at Columbia who looked after me. I told my son it is nothing to worry about and consulted Dr Mancini who reassured me that more work is being done all the time and there is a good chance that nothing will go wrong. But the risk is there.

'The condition means that the gene is not working in

the way that it should do,' says Dhairya, displaying utter calm when talking about the condition. 'It is as if there is a book with 1,000 words in it and one of those words has been spelt wrong. My heart works fine for now.' Dr Mancini has in fact suggested that Dhairya starts taking some medication now, but he has resisted this idea, because he says it will make him feel abnormal. For now he is opting for lifestyle changes instead, something in which he is supported by Dr Oz, who does not feel he should start taking medication yet.

Dhairya suspects that in a strange way I knew about his condition before he found out about it himself. I was the first person he told and, although he could sense I was extremely upset, I dealt with it in the best way I could, asking questions and assuring him that this was just a predisposition, not at all a certainty that anything would go wrong. But Dhairya was also desperately concerned about the rest of the family's reaction and how he should break it to his wife Karina. So I suggested that the four of us – Anita, Dhairya, Karina and I – should get together in the office the next day, as Anita also hadn't yet learned the news. I was the person to break it to them. 'My mother was devastated. Karina went into shock and then started crying,' Dhairya recalls, bravely focusing on a moment that was intensely difficult for all of us and it would be understandable if he wanted to forget it.

There is never a good time to tell anyone about these things but Karina felt it a particularly difficult blow because she was carrying Dhairya's second child at the time. 'Yes, I found out in the office when I was pregnant with my son,' says Karina, remembering with difficulty that dreadfully shocking period. 'I was very shaken up.'

And of course Bhanu was very worried about his brother: 'When I heard, my initial emotion was that it was all coming back again, after what happened to you and my uncle,' he says. 'But it is better to know because we can manage our lives better and there are plenty of people who specialise in these things, who we see and who can help all of us.' Bhanu himself is extremely health conscious, at one point a state champion in sprinting, show jumping and dressage and playing polo. He still spends time in the gym, runs and boxes and is self-disciplined, drinking in moderation and confining himself to the very occasional cigar. 'Of course I am concerned about my own children too but we have constant check-ups and I can deal with it now,' he says.

But it is Dhairya who has to deal with this now and, just as I first learned of my heart condition when I was a child, so he too grew up in the knowledge that heart disease is part of our family's history and that there is a chance it might one day affect him. 'Years ago I was told I would be tested one day,' he says. 'At that point the genetics was still very new but Dr Mancini said we would look when we had the correct tests and we have them now. I had the test at Columbia, and while I was shocked initially, between what happened to you and my uncle, I have also become a little desensitised to life. I'm not always open about my emotions. I always knew this was a possibility and I suppose deep inside I somehow knew this would be the case. I exercise more now and Columbia is keeping track of me: I will have an echo scan every six months and three years on, if they think there has been any further orientation, they will do extra tests. Now I feel I have to focus on my wife and children because I don't want them to go through what my mother and brother went through. I am being guided by my wife.'

Dhairya and Karina met at the end of 2007 and married in 2009. They have two children; Devina, who was born in 2011 and Shiva, who was born in 2014. Karina had not been on the scene when I went through my own operation, although, of course she learned about it as she and my younger son got closer, but now she was confronted with the reality of dealing with the same problem one generation down, in her own husband. She immediately began to acquaint herself with the condition to see what she could do.

'I started to study nutrition and epigenetics through Cornell,' says Karina. 'I really believe in the power of science and medical research and I feel that as the world advances, there will be some solution to this. There are also many doctors who practise lifestyle medicines now, and if you live your life correctly you can avoid getting predisposed to your genetic mutations. We have changed the food we eat: we avoid the wrong kind of oils, we eat red meat only once a week and Dhairya does not drink hard alcohol, just beer and wine. This is something I took over because I feel it's a blessing to know about it. In the beginning I was upset but I really look at it as a kind of awareness.'

Karina is as positive as Dhairya about the future but it is still the case that knowledge can be a burden. I have always known about my own heart condition but it has been extremely painful to see the next generation of my family having to deal with the same thing. Karina is firmly optimistic and is adamant that it is a blessing to have found out about Dhairya's condition. 'There's a science about eating correctly and, back in the day, people didn't have that awareness,' she says. 'I think now, if you have the awareness, you should take advantage of it.'

And of course the couple have children of their own. 'I'm not at all worried about it with my children because every time I go to the geneticists, every time I meet a doctor they say, "you shouldn't worry about your children, we can only do the gene test after the age of ten". Yet, I'm not worried about them at all in my heart. I'll worry about my husband, because I really believe, with the way research is going, a decade or two later, there will have been tremendous advancements for this specific type of mutation. I'm quite positive and recommend that people have genetic tests – not just for mutations, because we all have genetic predispositions and you might come out with things where you haven't had a disease in the family but you might have "this and this and this". Then you can go through life living with that thought, and one day it might become a reality. I think it's a great thing, especially for serious illnesses. I think a lot of people have gone through a journey like that and I think it's harder and very difficult for the carers and family who go through this.'

In some ways, it can even be as difficult for the loved ones of the person with the problem as it is for the person themselves. I know Anita went through hell when my own problems came to the fore and now I am also in the position of feeling heartache of a different sort, that of the father so terribly concerned about his son. But while doctors these days don't perform actual miracles, they can certainly work marvels, as I know from my own personal experiences and from meeting other heart transplant patients, which I will touch upon later in this book. It is difficult, though, when you want to give your children the best future possible, to learn that they might have issues associated with something so deep in your own and your family's past.

Certainly my own family – both my generation and the

ones that preceded it – have had experience of having to cope with a great deal and it took some thought on my part as to whether I would include this episode in our family's story in this book. Initially, I was reluctant. Although close members of the family knew about it the wider world did not, and I am only writing about it because Dhairya himself was adamant that I should do so and that he is perfectly happy for this information to become public and known to the wider world. 'It's not a secret,' he says firmly. 'There's absolutely nothing to hide.' As to whether it has cemented the bond between us, we already had an extremely close relationship, but Dhairya feels that it has given him an insight into what I had to go through. 'It opened my mind and I could see things through your perspective a lot more,' he says.

Dhairya's positivity is an object lesson in how to live your life, utterly admirable and inspiring to anyone. 'I'm glad I know about it,' he says. 'I can make a difference through lifestyle issues. I know I want to stay focused and dedicated to my goals, which are to have a happy marriage, to watch my kids grow up and make their way in life and to succeed and live as long as I can. I want to leave a legacy for my children and family.' Of course, Dhairya is concerned that these issues might affect his own children but, like Karina, he is resolved not to brood about it and points out, as she does, that medicine is advancing all the time.

CHAPTER 15

FATHER TO A COMPANY

When you are at the heart of a real crisis it can sometimes be difficult to see how it affects those around you and how your own travails have a real impact on their everyday lives. Of course, I knew that my family was desperately worried about what was happening to me and I was equally concerned about the stress and unhappiness it was putting on them. But it was only afterwards, as life began to return to normal, that the full magnitude of what had happened to me and everyone around me began to sink in. Sometimes it came out in ways that might almost sound trivial, events that seem perfectly normal on the face of it but that really mark a huge emotional turning point that might not even have been apparent at the time.

My nephew Dhruv recalled one of these, a seemingly

minor interaction between us of a type that had happened many times before but which now seemed to take on a huge significance, and which has lost none of its impact even though a decade and a half has passed since then. Some months after the surgery, the two of us were strolling through London's Green Park, a moment that to onlookers seemed simply like an uncle and his nephew talking about business but was in fact charged with emotion. We were away from hospitals, emergency rooms and the battery of medicines that had become my everyday life. We weren't talking about recovery periods or health awareness or anything whatsoever to do with the dual crisis that had affected my family, the death of Rajiv followed so quickly by my own illness. Everything was simply perfectly ordinary and normal and all the more blessed for that.

'You were talking to me about work,' says Dhruv now. 'You were saying, "You have to do this and you have to do that." And I just remember a tremendous feeling of happiness that it was going to be all right. You were recovering and you were out and about. I will never forget that walk.'

But it was not just my immediate family that had been affected. Company-wide, the news of Rajiv's death and my subsequent illness could not but have affected everyone who worked with us, that everyone at the top of the firm was working hard to alleviate, but which was almost inevitable. After all, a lot of people spend more time at work than they do with their families these days and, if the founders of a company become ill, it is only natural that many people employed by the company will feel personally affected.

This is when the top tier of management came into its own in the company, worrying about me while doing everything they could to keep the business focused. I had always motivated and encouraged my close colleagues and employees to be bold and to feel that they could surpass, their targets, and this both sustained them and drove them on when I had to go away; it also gave them the sheer will and determination to be there for everyone from the most senior managers to the humblest of the workers. We were both an actual family in the form of the Choudhries, but also an extended family in the form of the business, and all of these various obligations had to be looked after.

But two crises at the top of the company, affecting two figures so close together, were bound to have an impact. As I have mentioned earlier, Arun was particularly badly affected by Rajiv's death. 'It had a very deep impact on me. For a while, I lost all my confidence and sense of security,' he says. But he also later told me that my own illness had had a deep impact on many. 'You were a father figure in the company,' he tells me now. 'People who worked in a team with you were exceptionally close and would look to you for support so when this happened so soon after Rajiv there was an enormous sense of insecurity. For many of us, it was like a bad dream. But we had such a sense of responsibility that, when you were away, we were on our toes more than ever because you had trained us to hold ourselves together and be strong in your absence.'

At first only my closest associates knew that I was undergoing a heart transplant but, inevitably, the news spread to others after a while and, given that the procedure was all but unheard of in India at the time, there was a further sense of unease. But as soon as it became apparent that the operation had been a success, we made the news public to the company.

I later discovered that some people had even feared that I had died and, when I reappeared in India some months later, some business associates were so relieved that they rushed over and hugged me. I wasn't supposed to have too much physical contact with people in those early days – that ever-present risk of infection put paid to that – but some people were just so overcome with emotion they couldn't help themselves. Of course I didn't mind. I was absolutely delighted to see them too.

But it wasn't so surprising and when I look back to that time it is noticeable more and more that people's sense of apprehension and consternation about what was happening was compounded by how it came so soon after what had happened to Rajiv.

But while this story revolves around hearts – my old

heart and my new heart – many other hearts have been touched by this tale as well. Rajesh, married to my cousin Vandana, says, 'At first I didn't know about the history of heart disease in the family, but I became aware of it from the early 1990s onwards. It wasn't discussed very widely but I learned that both brothers had some issues and of course I learned much more when Rajiv became ill.

And then, of course, came my own illness, although Rajesh does tell me that looking at me he would never have guessed I'd had a transplant. 'I've hardly seen a difference in you but I don't know how you cope with the dietary restrictions, the fear of infection and the constant check-ups – it's amazing,' he says. 'And you still have the power of concentration: I have never seen you distracted. This has never affected your ability to make decisions and nor has it changed your incredibly positive attitude. I still worry whenever I know you're going for a check-up: in the early days, I used to wait for the phone call to come through to say you were all right and it was always a great relief.'

Even now, to this day, the members of my close-knit staff worry about me and when it comes time for my check-ups, they become a little tense and are relieved when they are given the OK. One of my staff, who has been with us for a number of years now, has actually said to me, 'You are very much the father figure within a family business. I know your own family is more important to you than anything and you've always shown interest in the rest of us, asking about my own two boys and taking an interest in us all rather than just appearing as the boss.'

It is touching to hear these words and heartening also to see how the business has grown and expanded since then. It is also impossible to say for certain quite how much of a role my health problems played or didn't play in the running of the company, although I suspect that it was not a great deal. But it is particularly pleasurable to hear people talk as if we have been one big family, not just a corporation, and one in which one towering family member will never be forgotten, despite having been taken from us so early. And the warmth with which people talk about him speaks for itself. My own health and the company's success are all a tribute to that force of nature that was my brother, my dear Rajiv.

CHAPTER 14

TO GIVE IS GREATER THAN TO RECEIVE

What greater gift can a person make than to give you their heart? Whether it is literally or emotionally, a heart is the essence of our being – literally at the heart of the body and emotionally at the heart of our lives. A twenty-year-old person from the Midwest whose identity I will never know not only gave me a new heart: they gave me a new life. They restored me to the heart of my family, to the people I love; they gave me, at the time of writing, sixteen years I would not have had otherwise. What can you say in response to a gift like that?

In the immediate aftermath of the operation, the hospital told me that like other heart transplant patients I could write to say thank you to the donor's family and put as much information as I would like in this letter. Of course I did so. The letter goes through the relevant doctor who passes it on to the family and if the family wants to reply to it they can do so. In this case the family chose not to and we never heard back from them, and of course no-one knows how they would feel and react if they were actually in that situation. But that precious gift the donor and his family made to me beats with emotion at the thought of what they did and what all heart donors and their families do for the people like me, who are, literally, given the means by which we can continue our lives.

I feel I owe it to that donor and to other heart donors and those needing transplants to try to do as much as I can to share my experience and knowledge, because despite the fact that this is now a very well-established procedure, it is still surrounded by a great deal of fear and ignorance, which will only start to disappear when people like me talk about it and explain exactly what it was like. Since my operation, both in the immediate aftermath and during the numerous visits I have made to Columbia since then, I have met many other heart transplant patients and I talk to as many as possible to tell them about my own experiences to show them that it is entirely possible to make a full recovery, even if it is with some restrictions on lifestyle, and to live a full life. Indeed, in many ways my quality of life is better now than it was in my late forties, when I was feeling lethargic, and constantly prone to infections as my health and my old heart gradually started to break down.

Just look, as so many people have repeatedly observed, what has happened to my appearance. I boast a full head of hair which even now strikes some people as different from the way I used to look. But that of course is the least of it: the best is to try to offer encouragement and reassurance, which is one of the purposes of writing this book. Heart transplants are major operations and a brutal assault on the body, but we are remarkably resilient creatures and life can hold more than ever once we have emerged from the other side. So much is important in terms of taking care of your body and making the most of a new lease of life, but perhaps the most important thing of all is a positive attitude. I was born with this and I have always looked on the bright side in any situation but never did it stand me in as good stead as it did when I needed a new heart.

I try to encourage this in other people, some of whom can be very taken aback to hear my story. On one occasion in the hospital, I went to meet a couple from Turkey: he was in his late sixties and due to have the operation and he and his wife were both clearly terrified. That is a very understandable reaction but I wanted to help in any way that I could. 'You mustn't worry about it,' I said.

'What are you talking about? How would you know?'

asked my fellow transplant patient, clearly believing I would not be able to understand what he was going through.

'I've had a transplant myself,' I told him.

The man looked utterly astonished to hear this. 'But you seem to eat normally. You look perfectly all right,' he said. I am perfectly all right, I told him and so when that man was wheeled into the operating theatre, he would at least know for a fact that he'd met someone who had survived and prospered and perhaps he would have felt more positive about the procedure he was about to undergo. And perhaps that positivity could have made a difference in the speed and extent of his recovery. You never know.

A small percentage of people who need transplants have other problems that they will need treatment for as well, so they get even more scared and they need to meet people who have been through it more than ever. Even now, although the first human heart transplant was performed by Christiaan Barnard in 1967 in Groote Schuur Hospital in Cape Town, the idea of taking a temporarily still organ from one body, the donor and reinstalling it, beating vigorously, into another patient, still can seem an almost impossible concept to comprehend.

The heart is symbolic in a way that other organs are not: the concept of the heart is so bound up with our sense of self in every culture that a heart transplant can be an emotional experience in a way, say, a kidney transplant is not. Hearts define personalities and emotions; kidneys are merely organs with a specific function, albeit an important one. My aunt Meenakshi Choudhrie, who was married to my late uncle Inder, had always been aware that there was a history of heart disease in my family, but expressed what so many in India thought at the time: 'How can a heart be replaced?' she asked. 'It seemed so strange. But when you came back to India months later, we realised it really would be OK.'

Bhanu feels very strongly about the fact that we need to demystify this operation and spread the word that there is life after a heart transplant – decades of it if you're lucky. 'The fact that you are a living example of someone who has been through it, who has displayed a determination to live and survive and be with your family, gives a lot of hope to people,' he says. 'It's important to get that message out to as many people as you can.' That is one of the reasons I decided to write this book: to show that there is life beyond the operating table. I myself have met inspirational people who have had a transplant and whose attitudes and ambitions have been breathtaking, taking on challenges that even people in perfect health would find daunting. After my own operation I met a woman in her thirties or forties who, post-transplant, was running a marathon, clearly a personal challenge to herself to show that she was, if anything, even healthier than she had been before her transplant. That really encouraged me.

But equally, I have met people who have had the operation, only to throw away the opportunities they have been given by adopting a negative and pessimistic attitude, which was in turn bound to have a bad effect on their recovery. Once I was in a room with six other transplant patients, and they were saying that they didn't want to do anything to protect their health as they didn't expect to live for very long. One man I met would not give up junk food – pizza – despite it being so clearly detrimental to his health: 'Why should I?' he said. 'I'm going to die anyway.' But as I am here to prove, that is simply not true. Ultimately we're all going to die anyway, but that fate can be delayed if you look after yourself properly. If you are fortunate enough to receive top quality medical care, as I did, then you have every chance of making it through.

I have wanted to do everything I can for Columbia and the field of heart surgery generally and while that partly involves talking about my own experiences, it also involves material and practical gestures as well. This is not a new part of my life: I grew up in a wealthy family and have had a long history of charitable giving. Call it noblesse oblige or what you will, but I was brought up to believe that if you yourself are fortunate, then you should do your bit for people who are not.

As I mentioned earlier in this book my mother brought us up to believe we should give something to society and she did a great many things, among them giving support to an orphanage, marking my father's birthday with further charitable work and giving to a blind school, which is something she began after my own eye was injured. She also gave support to spiritual institutes like the Ramakrishna Mission, where the family sought spiritual discipline and philosophy. This established a link between my personal medical problems and later supporting the institutions that helped which I would continue in later life. This tradition of philanthropy has become extremely important to me and as an adult I have been involved in a great many charitable initiatives. These have included donating to Sightsavers, the British Heart Foundation and Cancer Research, all of which are causes that have personally touched my life, while over in India we have done a great deal of work. This does not all have to be po-faced and serious: we have tried to make raising funds and charitable awareness enjoyable – for example, among much else, we have organised charity cricket matches to promote health campaigns. We also support the GG2 leadership and diversity awards, one of which recently went to Malala Yousufzai, the Pakistani schoolgirl shot by the Taliban because of her insistence on having an education.

Anita comes from a similarly philanthropic background from me and, as soon as we married, she began doing a great deal of work on her own. As this work has grown and expanded, so Anita has established a reputation as a hard-working and effective campaigner, who has done an enormous amount in the charitable sector. In 2005, drawing on her many decades of experience, she founded the charity Path to Success. This has a diverse set of aims including providing education for those who would not otherwise receive it, helping individuals with disabilities, long-term health concerns and limited financial resources and the provision of overseas aid and relief in the event of natural disasters. Bhanu, Dhairya, Simrin, Karina and Anita's brother Anil are all involved and I am very proud to say that the charity, and specifically Anita, have received numerous awards.

These awards have included Editor's Award Philanthropist of the Year by Asian Achievers Awards in 2013, the Globe Charity Champions awards in 2012 and the Globe Award in 2010 in honour of Anita's outstanding charitable work. This has encompassed, amongst other things, raising money for wheelchairs in an initiative called '60 for 60' to give to sixty NHS hospitals across England to mark the Queen's Diamond Jubilee in 2012. Anita is also a patron of the Amar Jyoti Charitable Trust, a pioneer patron of Learning Matters India and a patron for Age Care, which is based in New Delhi, amongst a great deal else. The younger generation are also heavily involved.

Our family thus comes from a long-standing tradition of philanthropy and so of course I wanted to become involved with the institution that had done so much for me. This has been the source of a great deal of personal fulfilment amongst much else besides. Soon after my surgery I became heavily involved with Columbia hospital in other ways that I hope would benefit both the institution itself and the people who go there to be treated. I am not doing this so much out of gratitude as a sense that I benefited from past research and now I want to help fund the research and treatment that will save people's lives in the future. It was the charismatic Dr Mehmet Oz who initially suggested that I become involved in Columbia in a more formal way and it has since been heartwarming to do what I could.

Our plans were first mooted in 2008 and in August 2009, just over a decade after my transplant operation, I helped Columbia to establish the Sudhir Choudhrie Professorship of Cardiology in Medicine at Columbia University Medical Center. The first holder of this post could not possibly have been more suitable for the position: my doctor and my friend Dr Donna Mancini, and the speech she gave when she acknowledged her appointment is reproduced at the end of this book.

Columbia has been generous in its response to our work for them over the years and Dr Lee Goldman asked me to include this following statement: 'CUMC has been very fortunate to have the Choudhries as partners and over the years the family has been very supportive of a number of key initiatives at the Medical Center. In 2008, Mr Sudhir Choudhrie established the Sudhir Choudhrie Professorship of Cardiology. Additionally, The Amrit Choudhrie Suite for Advanced Cardiac Care, located on the twelfth floor of the Presbyterian Building on the CUMC campus, was named in recognition of the family's longstanding support of Columbia's Advanced Cardiac Care Program. The Choudhrie family has recently made a generous major commitment for our new Medical and Graduate Education Building. This gift has been recognized with a named student lounge in the new building—The Choudhrie Family Foundation Student Lounge – which opened to students in the fall of 2016. Complementing the family's generosity, Sudhir Choudhrie serves on the CUMC Board of Advisors, and his sons Bhanu and Dhairya serve as members of the Children's Board at Columbia along with their wives, Simrin and Karina.'

The Amrit Choudhrie Suite for Advanced Cardiac Care, named in honour of my mother, seemed very appropriate. Given that she has personally suffered so much as a result of the heart ailments that afflicted members of her family, it seems only right that the place where other heart patients would be treated should bear her name.

My sons and I are now all on a board of about seventy non-fiduciary advisers to Dr Lee Goldman, who are not responsible for the day-to-day running of Columbia, but who are able to bring our expertise from hugely varying backgrounds to bear on the future of the hospital and the university. We are all aiming both to keep Columbia as an international centre of excellence which treats people from all over the world, and to support its dual role of maintaining the local community in Spanish Harlem, which is not a rich area and which needs help from outside. By participating in this way we are able to give Columbia the benefit of experience that members of the board have gained in different industries and from different countries worldwide.

Indeed, I'm not the only patient who wants to help to make a difference. 'It does happen that people join the board who have been treated here themselves, who have had friends or family who have been treated, or who are simply interested,' says Dr Goldman, going on to explain that this has an additional benefit in that it helps export expertise elsewhere, in our case to India. For various reasons medical schools in the US don't necessarily have many international affiliations in the way that, say, business schools do, and so just the presence of people from different cultures who are involved in the organisation means that additional centres of excellence can be fostered elsewhere by establishing relations with other cultures that wouldn't otherwise exist. 'If we didn't have people who are generous, we couldn't do what we do,' says Dr Goldman. He cites the goals of Columbia as producing cutting edge research, attracting the best students, providing the best clinical care and existing as an asset to the community. 'One of our key roles is to attract, mentor and retain the best calibre of people we can do,' he says.

Dr Goldman and I first met some years after my operation but of course he became aware of my family's history and our long-term relationship with Columbia from early on and felt that it was not only my own experiences but those of my brother that played a role in what I wanted to do. 'You were clearly very influenced by your brother's death and saw from that what good medical care can do,' he says. 'I also felt you had an appreciation both of your cultural heritage and what modern science can do.' Dr Goldman reiterates the fact that treating heart disease could never be a straightforward business: some people end up in hospital because of what they have done to themselves, while others, like me, were just there down to the luck (or otherwise) of the draw. 'Sometimes doctors say that one of the major ways to keep living a long and healthy life is to choose your parents well,' he says. 'Genetic heritage is the key to it all.'

And of course, if our contributions go towards finding out more about my own condition and what caused it then it will save future patients and their families from having to undergo the ordeal that we all did. 'As we do a lot of work in charity and funding science and medicine, then we can start looking into that area and funding that research,' says Bhanu, who has taken a very strong interest in the work Columbia does, mindful of the way in which this condition has affected his family. 'There are advances in medicine all the time.' Indeed, medical science is moving so fast that it is impossible to predict what the future holds for any of us but as Dr Goldman pointed out, heart transplants, while extremely traumatic procedures for the patient to go through, are becoming almost routine procedures, something that could not possibly have been envisioned a few short decades ago.

My links to Columbia have continued in other ways as well, not least in arranging for other members of my family to be treated in this centre of excellence, which offers the best possible chance of survival. In 2011 it emerged that my uncle Inder, my father's youngest brother, had developed pancreatic cancer. He died eventually but we did all we could to save him. His widow Meenakshi takes over the story: 'When you found out he was ill, you took over everything, getting in touch with all the US hospitals and eventually finding a doctor in Columbia,' she says. 'You arranged everything for us at a time when it was very difficult to think. It was a difficult and long surgery and the cancerous parts were removed but by then it had got into the bloodstream.' We arranged sessions of chemotherapy in London and Delhi and my uncle eventually returned to Columbia for treatment but by that time it had spread to the liver and in October 2013 he died. My aunt is generous with her description of that immensely difficult time, telling friends that I took over all the arrangements and postponed my own departure from Delhi as the death appeared imminent because I hadn't wanted her to be alone when it happened. 'The closeness within a family doesn't go away,' she says.

Family is important; so are the people you surround yourself with. I have treated my employees with generosity and in return I have received great loyalty. Once one of my employees actually confessed to stealing from the office – he was driven to this confession by his wife, who threatened to leave him if he didn't tell me what he had done. To the great astonishment of many of my colleagues I chose not to dismiss him. A colleague has remarked that he doesn't recall me ever firing anyone. But I gave that employee a second chance and I think it is safe to say that I have that man's loyalty for life.

If you expect the best of people then you might just end up with exactly that. Charity in both the public and the personal sphere underpins what makes us decent, moral beings, whether by contributing to the centre of excellence that is Columbia, or giving an errant employee a second chance. You can sense instinctively what people are like. It comes from the heart.

CHAPTER 15

A HEART'S DESIRE

Diwali in Delhi. Could there be a more beautiful time in what is still my spiritual home? My heart is American and my nationality these days is British, which is also where I have made my main base. But my soul is still Indian and during this beautiful time, the Festival of Light, I always try to visit New Delhi, where I still have a home, to reconnect with the ancient and mysterious civilisation from which I come.

Internationally, Diwali is probably the best known of the Indian festivals – and we have many – and it is a time of great hope and celebration. The whole of Delhi – and India – sparkles with the millions of strings of fairy lights that are arrayed over the public buildings, private homes and everywhere else and are left to sparkle for weeks, proclaiming the victory of light over darkness, knowledge over evil and good over despair. Private houses use coloured powder, rice, flour and flower petals to make Rangoli decorations, those colourful and intricate designs making patterns on courtyards and living rooms. Sometimes there will be archetypically Indian figures like painted elephants as decoration, with diyas – lamps and candles – everywhere, light and hope permeating every bit of our lives.

Diwali celebrations usually last about five days, but Diwali day itself is on the darkest new moon night of the Hindu month Kartika. We will hold a puja, or prayers, several times, where a pandit (priest) will officiate as we sing bhajans in praise of Lakshmi, the goddess of wealth and prosperity and ask for her favour in the year ahead. The first time we hold our prayers will be at the company offices in New Delhi and the second time will be in the family home in the evening, prior to a party when we will celebrate the festive season.

I have been taking part in these traditions since I was born and it is heartwarming to see my tiny grandchildren do likewise, their parents guiding them through the ancient rituals that link them to their forebears in the thousands of years of history in our ancient land. Their great-grandmother, my mother, is still able to participate in the ceremony, frail but so much a part of our rituals, drawing us closer still as a family, able to celebrate our happiness at being together after we have been through so much.

Then the party will start: champagne, fine wine and that drink much beloved of many Indians, whisky, will circle (though I will stick with water) as the family and guests glitter in their finery, enough to outshine the explosions of light outside. India is known for the brightness of its colours and the women will be resplendent in their saris, scarlet and peacock blue, emerald and pink, made of the finest silk and trimmed with lace. India is known for its magnificent jewellery, too, and stones will flash from the fingers of the women and occasionally, too, the men. Dinner will be served, prior to which we will all go outside to watch the magnificent firework display, individual to each household. Light has once more triumphed over darkness. The goddess Lakshmi has entered into our home.

Of course I grew up versed in the traditions of Hinduism, and worshipped and prayed throughout my life. Growing up, and as an adult in New Delhi, I attended a temple devoted to Hanuman, the god of protection, in Connaught Place, at the very heart of the city. Originally dating from around 1540 and reconstructed in 1724, the temple, which unusually has a spire with the form of a crescent moon (an Islamic symbol, not a Hindu one) is thought to be one of the five temples of the Mahabharata days in Delhi, thus dating back to around 400 years BC; its idol is Bala Hanuman, that is, Hanuman as a child.

That crescent moon, not a Hindu symbol, in some ways represents another aspect of my own spirituality, for while I am decidedly a Hindu, I could worship in a church, a synagogue or a mosque. There are many roads to God: I honour the one I was brought up in but I respect others too. But I do believe in reincarnation in the Hindu way. I have been going to the temple all my life: the special days of worship are Tuesdays and Saturdays and when I was at college I regularly attended on a Tuesday. My faith has been a gift to me: at times of great stress, and they have certainly existed, it has given me and the rest of the family strong moral support.

One holy man I have always followed is Sai Baba of Shirdi, a spiritual master who died in 1918 at the age of eighty-three and who was acknowledged as a saint as early as his teens. As I have said, although I am a Hindu, I could worship through many faiths and Sai Baba was remarkable in many ways, not least because it was never clear to his followers – and it still isn't – whether he was Muslim or Hindu himself. He himself said it was of no importance which he was: what mattered to him was that the individual surrendered himself to the satguru or murshid, the teacher who can lead the pupil to divine consciousness. An enigmatic figure, no one has ever been able to establish

Sai Baba's real name or where he was born: rather, when he first arrived at the town of Shirdi at around the age of sixteen years old, he was called 'Sai' by a local Muslim priest who recognised him as a saint.

His asceticism immediately marked him out from the ordinary and after a time he adopted the appearance for which he is now famous, wearing a Kafni robe and cloth cap. He received both Muslim and Hindu visitors and devotees and interpreted the religious texts of both those religions, speaking out strongly against judging individuals based on their religious convictions or caste – and because of him Shirdi has become an important place of pilgrimage. His teachings have meant a great deal to me. He is now worshipped all over the world.

In 2004 I became aware of another person who was to play a deeply important role in my spiritual life and indeed my physical one, for Anita firmly believes in Guruji, a saint from Punjab, who was born in in the early 1950s and passed away in 2007. A friend approached me and asked me to meet Guruji: I decided not to at the time but I did eventually donate funds to build a wall at his temple at the Bhatti mines in South Delhi, popularly known as Bade Mandir.

But it was Anita who met him first. 'Members of our family had been talking about him for some time and I had thought I would go to meet him but it never happened,' she recalls. 'However, in June 2006 I went and from the moment I entered the meeting place my mind and body were both hit by a powerful spiritual connection. It was as if my soul was reaching out and some kind of light was shining on me. He only spoke a couple of sentences to me but he said, "You have come after eleven years and so many days." He also said my name. I checked this with my sister and realised that I had met a very spiritual person from Punjab over eleven years previously, but I had had no recollection of it. He remembered it all.'

Anita became a regular visitor to Guruji's temple where people came to see him from all over the world. Tea and langar prasad (blessed food with his own divine blessings) would be served, both of which had great healing qualities. When Anita told him that my hip was going to be replaced, Guruji told her not to worry; she also took Dhairya to meet him and although our younger son was initially a little reluctant, Guruji told him that he must eat this blessed food and that through him blessings would be passed on to me.

Shortly before my hip operation, Anita had a spiritual experience which she is certain contributed to the unusually short operation and my very speedy recovery. One night, just as we were falling asleep, Anita felt a presence in our bedchamber which she knew was in some way Guruji. 'My heart was beating so loudly I thought I would faint,' she says. She experienced this for 10 or 15 seconds, but just as she fell into a deep sleep, 'I felt the presence going across to your side of the bed. Subconsciously I knew he had come to heal you and in the morning, not only did you feel better, but there was a fragrance of roses in the room, the sign of the presence of a saint.'

The operation still had to be done but it was much faster and even more successful than anyone could have predicted. Anita had put a picture of Guruji by my bedside in the hospital and when the doctor came in he noticed it at once. 'Who is this?' he asked. 'I have seen him before – I see a godly man.' In actual fact the two had never met but Anita believes that the doctor too might have felt Guruji's presence or experienced him as a flash in the mind. Guruji himself is now gone but his temple remains open, dispensing langar prasad and carrying a deeply spiritual and beneficial influence out into the wider world. Anita and the children wear his pendants and Anita still attends the prayer meetings of this modern saint.

Anita and I have both had our janampatri, or birth horoscopes, drawn up – and of course I studied astrology myself when young – but above all we have come to believe in destiny. Throughout all the turmoil we have endured, neither of us ever thought it was my destiny to die in that operating theatre and members of my extended family feel the same. Sometimes when they have asked each other why, in such similar circumstances, my beloved brother Rajiv died but I survived, that is the only answer they can come up with. Are our fates marked out for us before we are even born? I believe they are.

But this aspect of life is as important to me as any material success has ever been and so when an opportunity arose for me to open up a spiritual channel for a wider community I leapt at the chance. My whole family were involved and this too became a project and an occasion that drew us all closer together. Anita and I have always been extremely spiritual individuals and so when the company acquired some land in Karnal in the state of Haryana, on which we began to plan a development known as Alpha International City – a residential area covering 350 acres which will include houses, shops and schools – we realised this was the ideal moment and place to endow our own temple. And in February 2015, all the members of the family gathered for the inauguration of the Shiv Shanti Temple dedicated to Lord Shiva.

The temple is a typical Indian design. As you come in you see a shrine to Lord Ganesh, the god with the face of an elephant, on the left while on the right there is Goddess Durga sitting on a tiger. Going up to the front there are three shrines: to the left Lord Krishna and Radha and to the right Lord Hanuman carrying a Gada (mace). In the middle is a shivling, or lingam, representing Lord Shiva,

226

a symbol of the fact that the Holy Ganges flows through him. There is a receptacle to show that water is flowing through his head. There are three figures placed in the background: Lord Shiva's wife Parvati and his two sons Lord Ganesh and Lord Kartika, the war god with six heads, to correspond to the five senses and the mind. In front of him there are offerings for puja: supari (betel nuts), spices, sweets, flowers, fruit, milk, sugar, curd, rice and honey.

In India no one can own a temple, but we can facilitate its construction and maintain it, as well as paying for the three pandits, who live just outside the temple and spend the day there from 6am to 11am and then again from 5pm to 9.30pm. It has to shut at some points as God also must sleep. Anyone can come in to pray: against a background of music which plays continuously through the day, a chorus praising the gods, people can come in and ring the bell hanging above the hall, an action meant to clear the mind in order to pray. The floor of the temple is made of marble, as are the lower walls; the upper walls are constructed of the pink stone so typical of Jaipur.

There are collection boxes on either side of the main shrine so that visitors to the temple can also make their contribution, not just to the upkeep of the building but to the spiritual purpose it serves: the temple is there to function for the growing community and as the town grows up around it, so it will play its own part in the life of the people who live nearby. On festival days the pandits will perform the puja and they will also do so for people who visit especially, no matter what their own religion. If I can worship in temples, mosques and churches, then the temple that my family and I have endowed is equally open to those of all religious faiths. And this temple has meant a great deal to me as a part of wanting to do what I could for others, including those who suffer illness and pain themselves. Just as I wanted to make a material gesture towards medical research and the alleviation of suffering in the form of the various charitable initiatives I outlined in the last chapter, so I wanted to make a spiritual offering as well and this temple is one way of doing so, as is following my saint and holding on always to the notion of what is really important in life. What is all the wealth in the world without this spiritual aspect of our lives?

What have I learned from all this? That with world-class medical care you can recover from seemingly insurmountable health problems, that a positive attitude and a determination to accept the blessing of a new heart and live a life that is worthy of it are crucial to survive. But ultimately, I have learned that you must accept your destiny. Neither Anita nor I believed it was my destiny to die in that operating theatre and in the event we were right. Not that I would wish the experience of having a heart transplant on anyone: it is a searing experience to live through and the only thing that can really be said of it is that it's a lot better than the alternative. Someone once asked me what the word 'heart' meant to me: my immediate response was 'life'. They asked the same question to Dhairya: he immediately replied, 'Dad.'

Of course, at the heart of it all, this is a love story. Hearts have broken in this tale – more than one of them, and emotionally as well as physically – but they have been mended too. The hearts belonging to the family of my donor must have been shattered by their loss and yet they rose above their grief to say yes to the procedure that gave me life. My heart, my new heart, swells with a profound emotion at that thought.

And more than that: some hearts in this story have flourished. And my heart, my old heart and my new one, are both dedicated in every way they can be to Anita, my wife, my soulmate and my heart's desire. I had one heart before it gave out on me, I was lucky enough to be the recipient of another, but I gave both of them, quite freely, over and again to Anita. What will the future hold for my new heart or indeed for any of us? It's impossible to say, only to hope and to pray and to live the best life that all of us can live, no more. And still my heart beats on, in this dance with the music of time.

WITH THANKS

To my doctors – Dr Donna Mancini and
Dr Mehmet Oz.

And to my family, who have been there for
me and always will be there for me.

DR DONNA MANCINI'S SPEECH – TENTH ANNIVERSARY OF SUDHIR'S TRANSPLANT

Tonight is a night of celebration. The first celebration is to commemorate the ten-year anniversary of Bunny's heart transplant, and the second is the development of the Choudhrie Professorship.

So many of the transplant patients have very dramatic and inspiring stories. Young men and women who tragically developed end-stage heart disease but, with the advances of modern medicine, are now able to lead productive lives. The management of end-stage heart failure has markedly progressed over the last twenty years. When I first began my sub-specialty fellowship with Dr. Thierry Lejemtel, ACE inhibitors and Cyclosporine had just completed clinical trials. Use of beta blockers was contraindicated for heart failure. Patients with advanced heart disease lived a few months to, at most, two years. It is thrilling to witness the advancement in the therapy of this disease. The survival of patients before and after transplant has increased tremendously. It is amazing that I have been caring for some patients with dilated cardiomyopathy for over twenty years and they continue with good quality of life.

The management of end-stage heart failure patients is truly multi-disciplinary. Every week at 7am my surgical colleagues, fellow cardiologists, nurses, psychiatrists, neurologists, pulmonologists, infectious disease specialists, social workers, administrators and others meet to discuss in-depth problematic cases and determine the best medical and surgical options for these patients. These weekly transplant meetings are the central core for the organisation and functioning of our program. The animated discussions that frequently result raise questions that stimulate future research. The debates enable our group to reach consensus and move forward when we deal with difficult ethical issues. It binds the group together as it provides a forum for all our voices to be heard and respected. Over the years so many dramatic stories have been told and hundreds have literally been given new life and hope.

Bunny's case is no different. On Bunny's tenth-year anniversary I would like to review his case so you can all understand how truly miraculous this field is and how helping one man touches so many others.

Today may be the tenth anniversary of Mr. Choudhrie's transplant but my friendship with Bunny preceded his acute illness. In October 1997, I first met Bunny as a caring brother who was always at the side of his elder and only sibling Rajiv who was transferred to Columbia for a heart transplant evaluation. Rajiv was evaluated, listed and recovered sufficiently to return to Delhi and London but his recovery was short-lived. As his condition progressed, I advocated for a quick return to Columbia and initiation of intravenous support. However, the physicians in England referred his brother to the Cleveland Clinic for surgery. When I was informed of that decision, my heart sunk as this surgery was unproven and much too risky for such an ill patient. Rajiv's surgery did not go well, he required mechanical assist device support and died a few weeks [later,] never discharged from the clinic.

In January 1999, Bunny and I met again and now he was the patient with end-stage heart disease. Bunny had undergone mitral valve replacement in May 1997 and had a cardiac arrest for which he received an implantable defibrillator. His heart failure progressed and by the time he was transferred from NYU to Columbia he was rapidly failing. Though Bunny was transferred to the heart institute floor, he was quickly triaged to the coronary care unit where despite increasing intravenous support his condition continued to deteriorate. With this prior valve surgery, bridging Bunny to transplant with left ventricular assist device was not an ideal option. Fortunately Bunny is a blood type B which generally means shorter wait-times.

Miraculously on 17 January 1999 a donor heart from a twenty-year-old man from Michigan who was brain dead following a motor vehicle accident was identified. This was not an ideal donor. Many centres passed which was part of the reason it was so quickly available to us. The donor required thirty minutes of CPR and had a large fluid collection around the heart. This is where the art of medicine comes in and difficult decisions are made. The risk to the recipient with a possible contused organ needed to be weighed against the risk of waiting. Mehmet courageously dispatched a harvest team to Ann Arbor to inspect the heart. It looked normal. As the donor was young, the cardiac function was normal and on visual inspection of the heart, [it] looked good, Mehmet proceeded and performed successful surgery. The thrill of transplant never ceases to amaze me. To witness the sudden reversal of a downward spiral and literally snatch a patient from the jaws of death to begin a new life is awe-inspiring. I can still feel the joy that filled my heart when Mehmet called with the news of Bunny's successful transplant.

Bunny's post-operative course was complicated by

an unusual pneumonia which was diagnosed and well treated by my colleagues, Drs Lee, Scully and Schulman. Bunny grew stronger and returned to New Delhi and his international lifestyle. Fortunately, he experienced no rejections and his coronary arteries remain clear of obstructions. The years following transplant have been full of joyous celebrations of weddings, anniversaries, significant birthdays and graduations. Over the last ten years, Bunny has been a devoted father who has been able to watch both his sons mature into fine young men. Under his mentorship, both Bhanu and Dhairya have assumed increasingly large roles in the administration of his multiple businesses. Anita has always been at Bunny's side overseeing and caring so lovingly for him. Her watchful eyes have truly been instrumental in helping Bunny maintain his good health. Three years ago Anita noted that Bunny had intermittent left thigh pain; a few months later the diagnosis was clear that Bunny had developed avascular necrosis of his left hip from previous steroid therapy and required left hip replacement. Dr Macaulay performed a total hip replacement and in just a few weeks Bunny was back jetting around the globe. Both Bhanu and Daryiha enjoy teasing their mom on her attention to medical details and have awarded her an honorary MD degree but if their mom was a physician, she would be brilliant.

As Bunny now moves into the second decade with his

transplanted heart, I know he worries about the longevity of his heart. Life is full of clear and unforeseen dangers. For long-term transplant survivors the greatest danger to graft survival remains being lulled into a state of complacancy, neglecting their medical regimen and adopting unhealthy life styles. I have no fear that with Anita at your side this will not occur. May the next ten years bring you and your family many more joys. May your health continue to flourish so that you achieve your goals – opening of your hospital in New Delhi and London, your return to New Delhi, more marriages (Dhairya!) and the birth of grandchildren. Bunny you are a brilliant businessman with a gentle, generous and kind soul who deserves many more years of happiness. You have had enough tragedy for many lifetimes. May the future hold only joy.

Now in regard to the chair:

Bunny is an insightful businessman. He is aware that, though tremendous progress has been made in the management of end stage heart failure, there is still much work to be done. Today we have become very successful in slowing the disease process but the future holds the promise of not only delaying the symptoms of severe heart failure but developing treatment modalities that actually restore heart function. One of the most spectacular observations over my career was witnessing the complete reversal of heart failure in some patients supported by left ventricular assist devices, i.e. massively enlarged hearts that over time with mechanical and medical therapy are restored to normal function. These patients were thought to have irreversible disease but these cases demonstrated the ability of the heart to repair itself. These cases represent the hope that in the future we can devise treatments that not only palliates heart failure but cures it. Gene therapy, stem cell therapies are no longer science fiction but are becoming realities. The development of a Choudhrie professorship enables Columbia University to support basic and clinical research programs that will help to bring these therapies to fruition. The endowment generously provided by the Choudhrie family will grow over time and support not a single but several future professors.

I am overwhelmed at being named as the first recipient of this chair and to receive it on such a historic day. Today in Washington, a truly inspiring leader, Barack Obama, becomes our new president. The son of a black man, raised by a divorced white woman who began his career as a community organizer now leads the free world. And tonight a poor kid from the lower east side with a loving family receives an endowed chair from an Ivy League institution. These stories just prove that in America anything is possible with a lot of determination, a little intelligence and much passion.

One image comes to mind from the opening ceremonies

of the Beijing Olympics this past summer. A beautiful woman garbed in an Asian dress with robes blowing in the wind and ribbons streaming from her hands dances and whirls atop of an immense platform supported by hundreds of her fellow citizens. Not only was this image visually beautiful but its symbolism was strikingly powerful. Graphically it showed that her dance was made possible only through the support of others. Today I dance like that woman knowing I can only because of the support I have received from my colleagues, family, friends and mentors. This chair represents our collective accomplishments. Thank you, Bunny, for your generosity. Thank you all for each of your roles that made this day possible. May we continue to dance joyfully into the future.

January 2009

SUDHIR CHOUDHRIE PROFESSORSHIP OF CARDIOLOGY LECTURE BY DR. OZ

Good evening, Dean Goldman, friends and faculty.

I want to offer personal thanks to the Choudhries for their generosity to Columbia and for establishing the Sudhir Choudhrie Professorship of Cardiology.

Congratulations to my colleague Donna Mancini – a brilliant choice to be the first Sudhir Choudhrie Professor.

Donna arrived in 1993, kept us [as a] top tier program by designing famous formulas to tell which patients really needed a transplant, identifying and treating rejection faster than ever before, and serving as a tireless leader on our Friday morning transplant rounds. She fought for her patients and made tough moral choices like pushing for trials of the new drug sirolimus to delay the deadly chronic graft vasculopathy.

All through these experiences, she lost relatives and loved one[s] on our transplant list. But she always kept her head up, even learning to drive, although I am still nervous about her initial harrowing attempts to merge into high speed traffic for the first time in her compact car designed to match her compact body.

She allowed me to try unconventional approaches on our patients who were desperate for any opportunity to improve their quality of life. We used energy therapy for the first time and other alternative medicine approaches like audiotapes and massage.

Lisa and I have gotten to know and love Bunny and Anita Choudhrie, as well as their two wonderful sons Bhanu and Dhairya. I want everyone here to appreciate how special they are, so please allow me to offer some personal remarks about the family and highlight their thoughtful philanthropy in establishing an endowed professorship at Columbia.

Recently, they took my wife Lisa and I on a tour through India. We started in the majestic town of Rishikesh on the Ganges River where we saw Ashrams and wise gurus and heavenly throngs of pilgrims along this sacred river at the foot of the Himalayas. This source of energy powers this couple's desire to rise above the daily challenges of life and seek higher paths to changing our communities for the better.

We then toured the famous Golden Triangle of India covering three of the most beautiful and captivating cities of the country – Delhi (the capital of India), Agra (the city of Taj) and Jaipur (the land of Rajput kings). It is actually a kaleidoscope that presents the Indian pageantry in its most colourful forms and offers you a dazzling vista of stately and grandiose architectural buildings, forts and palaces with a legendary heritage and a fertile and affluent tradition of art and culture. These cities are undoubtedly the epitomes of Indian cultural, historical and architectural heritage and have all been the capitals of the princely states. The inherent elegance of this historic triangle parallels the beauty of this couple's relationship with each other and our broader community.

They know that charity does not prevent death, but it does prevent dying while you are alive. The Choudhries know that when we contribute, paradoxically, we grow as well. At our core, people seek significance in life rather than purpose and we find this most predictably through service. But perhaps most importantly, the Choudhries know that they need to heed Elie Wiesel's challenge, 'Have you asked a good question?' And they always ask great questions which is why we are here today. They have supported the creation of a special forces team for transplantation that is breaking down barriers daily.

Finally, leaders do not adapt to change but create it. The Choudhries have been encouraging us to create a vision that they have had since they first entered New York Presbyterian. Sam Walton encourages us to 'Do what you are big enough to do' and thankfully the Choudhries are plenty BIG enough to be the force behind change. But they offer an elegant insight similar to what I learned from a famous college basketball [coach] who grew up in a busy city. Coach was told by his mom to take the 'right' bus to school. He was starting at a new school, she argued, and he needed to make the right first impression. Picking the right bus was critical because only by getting on the bus could he be sure that he would be traveling with the right people. Only later did he realise that his mom was also speaking metaphorically about the bus of life. Riding with the right people makes a huge difference and I am honoured that the Choudhries are on our bus as we drive towards even greater success.

Lisa and I are delighted to be here this evening to celebrate Bunny's and Anita's great generosity to Columbia University Medical Center and to applaud Donna and her new title. It is a wonderful partnership.

January 2009

Who Owns the Future?